THE
WAR ON DRUGS
IS A
WAR ON FREEDOM

Books by Laurence M. Vance

The Other Side of Calvinism
A Brief History of English Bible Translations
The Angel of the Lord
Archaic Words and the Authorized Version
A Practical Grammar of Basic Biblical Hebrew
Double Jeopardy: The NASB Update
Christianity and War and Other Essays Against the
     Warfare State
King James, His Bible, and Its Translators
Greek Verbs in the New Testament and Their Principal Parts
War, Foreign Policy, and the Church
Guide to Prepositions in the Greek New Testament
The Myth of the Just Price and the Biblical Case for
     Laissez Faire
Guide to Nouns in the Greek New Testament
Guide to Adjectives in the Greek New Testament
Guide to Pronouns in the Greek New Testament
The Revolution that Wasn't
Rethinking the Good War
Galatians 1 & 2: Exposition, Commentary, Application
The Quatercentenary of the King James Bible
The War on Drugs Is a War on Freedom

THE
WAR ON DRUGS
IS A
WAR ON FREEDOM

by

Laurence M. Vance

Vance Publications
www.vancepublications.com

ISBN 978-0-9823697-5-3

Cover image by Paul Kolsti (1953-2003) used by
permission of Joseph Szabo of WittyWorld

Published and Distributed by: Vance Publications
P.O. Box 780671, Orlando, FL 32878
E-mail: vancepub@vancepublications.com
Website: www.vancepublications.com

Printed in the United States of America

TABLE OF CONTENTS

FOREWORD

It would be difficult to find a better example of a failed government program than the war on drugs. Not only has the drug war failed to stem the use of illicit drugs in American society; it has also allowed the federal government to gain vast power over the American people, at the expense of individual liberty. Moreover, in an era in which out-of-control federal spending and debt are of paramount concern to American taxpayers, U.S. officials continue to spend more than $40 billion a year to wage the drug war.

Just as the prohibition of alcohol during the 1920s led to the illegal production of booze and widespread violence at the hands of illegal alcohol producers, so it has been with the prohibition of drugs, which has led to drug cartels, gang warfare, murders, robberies, muggings, and official corruption. The entire 40-year history of the war on drugs is a testament to Santayana's famous dictum, "Those who cannot remember the past are condemned to repeat it."

In the pages of this book, Laurence Vance sets forth a persuasive case for ending the drug war on practical grounds. As most everyone acknowledges, this federal program just hasn't worked, and it's extremely destructive. Vance doesn't mince words:

> The federal war on drugs is undefendable. Not only has it failed to curtail drug use, it has eroded civil liberties, destroyed financial privacy, corrupted law enforcement, crowded prisons with non-violent offenders, ruined countless lives, and wasted hundreds of billions of taxpayer dollars.

The utilitarian case that Vance sets forth for ending the drug war, however, is not what sets this book apart. The power of this book is the moral case that Vance makes for totally legalizing drugs—all drugs.

Under what moral authority does government punish people for ingesting substances that the authorities consider harmful? How can such a power—the power to fine, incarcerate, and imprison a person for ingesting a harmful substance—be reconciled with the fundamental principles of individual liberty?

Freedom entails the right to engage in any behavior whatsoever, so long as it is peaceful. As long as a person isn't trespassing on the rights of others through violence or fraud, the principles of freedom entitle him to make whatever choices he wants in life, no matter how irresponsible, dangerous, or unhealthy they might be.

A society in which the government punishes people for actions considered self-destructive, irresponsible, or unhealthy cannot truly be considered a free society. It's not a coincidence that laws criminalizing the possession, use, or distribution of drugs are an integral part of such totalitarian regimes as those in Cuba, North Korea, China, and Myanmar.

Here is how Vance compares societies that are free with those that are not:

> In a free society the individual makes his own decisions about his health and lifestyle; in an authoritarian society the state thinks it knows best how to make those decisions. In a free society the individual is free to make bad decisions; in an authoritarian society the state thinks it knows best what decisions people should make....

> Philosophically, it is not the purpose of government to be a nanny state that monitors the behavior of its citizens. It is simply not the purpose of government to protect people from bad habits or harmful substances or punish people for risky behavior or vice. Drug prohibition is impossible to reconcile with a limited government.

One of the most fascinating parts of this book is chapter 16: "Should Christians Support the War on Drugs?" Because illicit drugs are considered bad, all too many Christians automatically conclude that the prohibition of such drugs should be rendered unto Caesar. Not so, argues Vance. There are some sins—specifically the ones entailing non-violent behavior—that do not legitimately fall within the realm of government control. Adultery, blasphemy, and covetousness come to mind. In fact, that the drug war has proven to be such a fiasco is persuasive evidence that God has created a consistent universe, one in which evil means beget bad consequences.

Vance also reminds us of the hypocrisy of drug prohibition. Alcohol and tobacco are much more destructive than, say, marijuana. Yet liquor and cigarettes are legal while marijuana is not. Why the difference?

Unlike many other opponents of the drug war, however, Vance doesn't limit his case to calling for the legalization of marijuana. He makes the principled case for the legalization of all drugs, arguing that the illegality of any drug not only produces destructive consequences but, more important, constitutes a grave violation of people's freedom to live their lives the way they choose.

What about the Constitution? Does it play a role here? Vance reminds us that the Constitution established a federal government of limited, enumerated powers. Is the power to punish people for ingesting harmful substances among those enumerated powers? It is not, which is why Americans had to seek a constitutional amendment to criminalize the possession and distribution of alcohol, an amendment that was later repealed owing to the horrible consequences of Prohibition.

Many of the articles in this book were originally published by The Future of Freedom Foundation, where I serve as president. Ever since our founding in 1989, we have taken a firm, uncompromising stance against the war on drugs. We have always held that the drug war has brought nothing but death, destruction, robberies, muggings, assassinations, corruption, drug gangs, domestic warfare, overcrowded prisons, wasted money, and ruined lives. More important, it has been one of the greatest governmental assaults on liberty and privacy in our nation's history.

We were pleased to have published Laurence Vance's powerful essays on the drug war when he originally submitted them to us, and we are just as pleased that they now form part of this powerful book, a book that should be read by every American who is concerned about the principles of morality, freedom, free markets, the Constitution, and limited government.

Jacob G. Hornberger
Founder and President
The Future of Freedom Foundation

INTRODUCTION

This is not a book about the benefits of drugs; this is a book about the benefits of freedom. I neither use illegal drugs nor recommend their use to anyone else. I am even skeptical about the health benefits of most legal drugs.

So why this book? Because I believe in freedom. I believe in individual liberty, private property, personality responsibility, a free market, a free society, and a government as absolutely limited as possible. I also believe that my perspective on this subject is unique.

The nineteen essays in this book were all written between October 2009 and July 2012. One was published in the journal *Freedom Daily*, another in the magazine *The New American*, one appeared online as a *Mises Daily* article, another was a column at LewRockwell.com, and the rest were first written as *Future of Freedom Foundation Commentaries*. Each essay is reprinted verbatim. The source and date of each essay is indicated below its title. Because the essays are arranged only in chronological order, each one can be read independently of the others. All the essays that originally appeared online had links to document my quotations and sources. These can easily be accessed online should the reader be interested. I would like to again thank the editors of the various publications who first published these essays.

The book's first essay, "The Drugs of John Gray" (the allusion to the title of the novel *The Picture of Dorian Gray* is intentional), although acknowledging that the philosopher John Gray makes a strong case for drug legalization, argues that his "unanswerable" argument is weak because it is not based on the freedom to take drugs for freedom's sake.

In "The Moral Case for Drug Freedom," I argue that it is neither the job of government nor the business of any individual to prohibit, regulate, restrict, or otherwise control what a man desires to eat, drink, smoke, inject, absorb, snort, sniff, inhale, swallow, or otherwise ingest into his body. And that there is no ethical precept in any religion or moral code that should lead anyone to believe that it is the job of government to do these things. I do not argue for the benefits of drugs, only for the benefits of freedom. A version of "The Moral Case for Drug Freedom" was first presented at the 2010 Austrian Scholars Conference at the Mises Institute in Auburn, Alabama.

"The Case against Medical Marijuana" is actually the case against demonizing a plant and for the legalization of all drugs on an equal basis. It was originally written after Proposition 19, the Regulate, Control & Tax Cannabis Act, was rejected by California voters in November of 2010.

The book's fourth essay asks the question: "Why Don't Conservatives Oppose the War on Drugs?" Here I point out that the reason conservatives should oppose the war on drugs is a simple one that has nothing to do with the failures and evils of the drug war. Drug prohibition by the federal government is simply unconstitutional. In fact, nowhere does the Constitution authorize the federal government to ban any substance. Conservatives who claim to revere the Constitution should be ardently opposed to the drug war on the federal level just as much as libertarians.

In "Drug-Warrior Hypocrisy," I maintain that the paternalism of statists is at its worse when it comes to the war on drugs. Drug warriors are hypocrites because every bad thing that could be said regarding drug abuse could also be said of alcohol abuse—and even more so. Yet, in spite of the negative effects of alcohol on morals and health, few Americans would like to return to the days of Prohibition.

In "The Drug War Is Expanding," I tackle the issue of the use of bath salts as a hallucinogen. It is no more the job of government to address this recent phenomenon than it is for the government to have anything to do with pot smoking or cocaine snorting. Once government is elevated to such a level that it is allowed to determine what people can and can't ingest, or regulate the circumstances under which something can be lawfully ingested, there is no stopping its reach.

"Baseball, Steroids, and a Free Society" was written after Barry Bonds was found guilty of obstructing justice in an April 2011 trial for his 2007 indictment. Here I argue that in a free society Major League Baseball would make its own drug policy and the government would not be involved in any way.

In "U.S. Attorneys Crack Down on the Tenth Amendment," I explain how the federal government, in cracking down on providers and users of medical marijuana in the states where it has been legalized, is actually cracking down on the Tenth Amendment. The crackdown on marijuana by U.S. attorneys is an attack on the Constitution, the Founding Fathers, the principle of federalism, and the very nature of our republic. Congress has been granted no power to ban, regulate, or otherwise interfere with the production, sale, distribution, possession, or use of marijuana for the simple reason that it has no authority over any drug.

In "Why Is the U.S. Fighting Mexico's Drug War?," I examine Mexico's war on drugs and how the United States is intimately involved in it. I conclude that the United States should not only stop funding and participating in the Mexican drug war, but likewise end the futile and destructive war on drugs in America.

"The 40-Year War on Freedom" is the account of how President Nixon declared a war on drugs in 1971. I also argue in this essay that the war on drugs is incompatible with a free society because once the government claims control over what a man smokes, snorts, sniffs, inhales, or otherwise ingests into his body, there is no limit to its power.

In "The War on Drugs Is Senseless," I discuss the new cigarette warning labels and conclude that *if* the government is going to make a harmful substance illegal, then it seems logical that that substance should be tobacco. The number of annual deaths caused by all drugs—legal and illegal—pales in comparison with deaths caused by tobacco.

In "The Other Unconstitutional War," I focus on the unconstitutionality of the drug war, but also point out many of its evils. The war on drugs has increased the size and scope of government. The war on drugs has served as a pretext for a war on individual liberty and private property. The war on drugs entails Soviet-style central planning by the federal government. No American who has any respect for the Constitution, federalism, and the limited government established by the Founders should endorse, support, or defend the federal war on drugs, regardless of his political persuasion, religion, or moral code.

"Drug Testing for Welfare Benefits" explores the absurdity of the whole idea. In a libertarian, that is, a free society based on voluntary cooperation and contracts instead of government coercion and regulations, both drug-prohibition laws and welfare benefits would be illegitimate.

In "Drug-Sentencing Disparities," I explain how sentencing for drug crimes is extremely arbitrary in nature. The solution to the madness that is drug sentencing laws is not to reduce some sentences and increase others in order to eliminate disparity and racism, but to eliminate any sentences for possessing or selling a substance the government doesn't approve of. It is a national disgrace that the United States leads the world in the incarceration rate and in the total prison population.

In "Three Views on the Drug War," I contrast the libertarian and prohibitionist views on the drug war, and the confusing mass of inconsistency, hypocrisy, and nonsense that lies between them. Individual liberty and personal freedom are the farthest things from the minds of partial prohibitionists who want the drug war to be altered in some way but not eliminated.

In "Should Christians Support the War on Drugs?," I ask and then answer the question in the negative. Christians shouldn't support the government's war on drugs any more than they should support the government's wars on poverty, obesity, dietary fat, cholesterol, cancer, and tobacco. Christians are making a grave mistake by looking to the state to legislate morality. Although drug abuse is a great evil, the war on drugs is an even greater evil. It is simply not biblical to promote legislation or crusades to punish sin that does not aggress against person or property.

In "The Drug War: Cui Bono?," I point out that some groups of people support the drug war because they have something to gain from it. I discuss how the drug war benefits drug dealers, alcohol distributors, the prison industry, law enforcement, and the federal Drug Enforcement Administration. I also mention physicians and the pharmaceutical industry, state and federal prosecutors, judges and lawyers, the CIA and the FBI, the drug-testing and addiction-recovery industries, and any group receiving federal funds for anti-drug campaigns.

In "Twelve Victims of the Drug War," I delineate twelve victims of the Drug War that are rarely considered: the Constitution, the English language, the American taxpayer, common sense, people who conduct business with cash, people with allergies, crime, law-abiding Americans, law enforcement, people who suffer with genuine pain, doctors who prescribe pain medicine, and individual liberty.

The last essay in the book, "Why the War on Drugs Should Be Ended," is a no-holds-barred defense of absolute drug freedom. There are many reasons for ending the drug war, and I even list twenty-six of them, but the drug war should not be ended simply for logical, pragmatic, and utilitarian reasons. I conclude that the war on drugs should be ended because it is a war on the free market, a free society, and freedom itself.

As long as there is a war on drugs, the essays in this book will remain timely. Yes, there is some repetition throughout the book. But this is because the evils of the drug war never change and because the hypocrisy of drug warriors is unrelenting. And in the end, it always comes down to the issue of property and freedom versus badges and guns

For further reading, I recommend the following books, but not necessarily everything in them that doesn't relate to the war on freedom known as the war on drugs:

Block, Walter. *Defending the Undefendable*. San Francisco: Fox & Wilkes, 1991.

Duke, Steven B., and Albert C. Gross. *America's Longest War: Rethinking Our Tragic Crusade Against Drugs*. New York: Jeremy P. Tarcher/Putnam, 1993.

Fish, Jefferson M., ed. *How to Legalize Drugs*. Northvale: Jason Aronson, 1998.

Fox, Steve, Paul Armentano, and Mason Tvert. *Marijuana is Safer: So Why Are We Driving People to Drink?* White River Junction: Chelsea Green Publishing Co., 2009.

Harsanyl, David. *Nanny State: How Food Fascists, Teetotaling Do-Gooders, Priggish Moralists, and Other Boneheaded Bureaucrats Are Turning America into a Nation of Children*. New York: Broadway Books, 2007.

Healy, Gene, ed. *Go Directly to Jail: The Criminalization of Almost Everything*. Washington DC: Cato Institute, 2004.

Huebert, Jacob H. *Libertarianism Today*. Santa Barbara: Praeger, 2010.

McWilliams, Peter. *Ain't Nobody's Business If You Do: The Absurdity of Consensual Crimes in a Free Society*. Los Angeles: Prelude Press, 1993.

Miller, Joel. *Bad Trip: How the War on Drugs is Destroying America*. Nashville: WND Books, 2004.

Napolitano, Andrew P. *It Is Dangerous to Be Right When the Government Is Wrong: The Case for Personal Freedom*. Nashville: Thomas Nelson, 2011.

Okrent, Daniel. *Last Call: The Rise and Fall of Prohibition*. New York: Scribner, 2010.

Silverglate, Harvey A. *Three Felonies a Day: How the Feds Target the Innocent*. New York: Encounter Books, 2009.

Stossel, John. *No, They Can't: Why Government Fails—But Individuals Succeed*. New York: Threshold Editions, 2012.

Szasz, Thomas. *Our Right to Drugs: The Case for a Free Market*. Westport: Prager Publishers, 1992.

Thornton, Mark. *The Economics of Prohibition*. Salt Lake City: University of Utah Press, 1991.

1

The Drugs of John Gray
(*Mises Daily*, October 6, 2009)

The government's War on Drugs, like its War on Poverty and its War on Terror, is a failure. It has clogged the judicial system, unnecessarily swelled prison populations, fostered violence, corrupted law enforcement, eroded civil liberties, and destroyed financial privacy. It has encouraged illegal searches and seizures, ruined countless lives, wasted hundreds of billions of taxpayer dollars, hindered legitimate pain treatment, and had no impact on the use or availability of most drugs in the United States.

As a consequence of this failed drug war, people from all across the political spectrum are now, more than ever, calling for some degree of drug decriminalization or legalization.

A recent example is political philosopher John Gray. In an article entitled "The Case for Legalising All Drugs Is Unanswerable," Gray makes a strong case for drug legalization. The worldwide war on drugs should be ended because

- The drug war has maimed, traumatized, or displaced uncounted numbers of people.
- In spite of it, drug use has remained embedded in the way we live.
- The costs of drug prohibition now far outweigh any possible benefits.
- Penalizing drug use drives otherwise law-abiding people into the criminal economy.
- Prohibition exposes drug users to major health risks.
- Illegal drugs can't easily be tested for quality and toxicity.
- A great many drug users in years past lived productive lives before drugs were banned.

- Drug users face inflated prices, health risks, and the threat of jail.
- Politicians who have used drugs have not suffered any significant political fallout.
- The extreme profit reaped from selling illegal drugs corrupts institutions and wrecks lives.
- The antidrug crusade in Mexico has escalated into something like low-intensity warfare.
- Some states have been more or less wholly captured by drug money.

He could also have pointed out, like many others have, that certain illegal drugs have proved effective in pain relief, that people who smoke marijuana have a decreased risk of certain diseases, or that prescription-drug abuse kills people (Elvis, Heath Ledger, Michael Jackson) just like illegal-drug overdoses do. He could have noted that alcohol abuse is a greater social problem than illegal drug use, or that there were 1,702,537 drug arrests last year in the United States alone, almost half for simple possession of marijuana.

The problem with Gray's "unanswerable" argument is that it is utilitarian. It is not an argument based on the freedom to take drugs for freedom's sake. If the drug war *stops* maiming, traumatizing, and displacing people, if the costs of drug prohibition become *less* than its benefits, if illegal drugs *can* be tested for quality and toxicity, if the low-intensity warfare in Mexico *ends*, etc.—then, according to Gray, the war on drugs might be a good thing.

The only unanswerable argument is the argument from the standpoint of liberty and freedom from government intrusion into one's personal life. Nowhere in his article does Gray even consider that it is neither the job of government nor the business of any individual to prohibit, regulate, restrict, or otherwise control what a man desires to eat, drink, smoke, inject, absorb, snort, sniff, inhale, swallow, or otherwise ingest into his body.

Whether drugs are used for medical or recreational use is of no consequence. And neither does it matter whether drug use will increase or decrease. A government with the power to outlaw harmful substances or immoral practices is a government with the power to ban any substance or practice. There should be no such thing as a controlled substance.

Conservatives who revere the Constitution should support both the freedom to use drugs for any purpose and a free market in drugs. Nowhere does the Constitution authorize the federal government to intrude itself into the personal eating, drinking, or smoking habits of Americans. Indeed, before the Harrison Narcotics Tax Act of 1914, there were no federal drug laws in the United States.

John Gray warns against a "libertarian utopia in which the state retreats from any concern about personal conduct." But that is not what we need to be concerned about. It is puritans, busybodies, nannies, and other statist do-gooders—in and out of the government—who are the problem.

The drugs of John Gray are regulated, licensed, taxed, monitored, and otherwise controlled. But without a real free market in drugs, drug legalization is really nothing but state control of the drug market, as Thomas Szasz has pointed out.

John Gray's case for legalizing all drugs is answerable; it is the case for liberty that is unanswerable.

2

The Moral Case for Drug Freedom
(Freedom Daily, August & September 2010)

My title is a radical one, and deliberately so.

There is a reason I did not say, "The Moral Case for Drug Legalization," or, "The Moral Case for Drug Decriminalization," or, "The Moral Case for Drug Regulation," or, "The Moral Case for Medical Marijuana," or, "The Moral Case for Relaxing Drug Laws," or, "The Moral Case for Ending the Drug War." My title is also a positive one. If I were going to give it a negative title I might have said something like:

The Moral Case Against Religious Restrictionists
The Moral Case Against Pious Prohibitionists
The Moral Case Against Christian Crusaders
The Moral Case Against Fundamentalist Fascists
The Moral Case Against Puritanical Prudes
The Moral Case Against Nondenominational Nazis
The Moral Case Against Evangelical Extremists
The Moral Case Against Bible-Believing Busybodies
The Moral Case Against Meddling Moralists

I want to present the moral case for drug freedom.

In the 15 or so years that I have been writing as a conservative Christian libertarian, and certainly not before that, I had never written anything, until last October for *Mises Daily*, exclusively about the subject of drugs. I hesitated to do so not because I had only recently came to the conclusion that the war on drugs was a monstrous evil. To the contrary, I can remember questioning the whole idea of drug prohibition and victimless crimes when I was just, for lack of a better term, a libertarian-leaning conservative. My hesitation in writing anything negative about drug prohibition was due to the pathetically predictable negative reaction I knew I would receive outside of libertarian circles, and especially due to the hysterical reaction I knew I would receive from some of my conservative Christian brethren.

The defenders of drug prohibition would argue:

- I was in favor of drug abuse.
- I was a liberal.
- I was a libertine.
- I was a pragmatist.
- I was promoting the breakdown of society.
- I was ignorant of the harmful effects of drugs.
- I was sending the wrong message to young people.
- I was denying established cultural norms.
- I was focusing on money instead of morality.

Drug prohibitionists who consider themselves religious would argue likewise and add:

- I was advocating situation ethics.
- I was giving up on family values.
- I was compromising with the world.
- I was undermining Christian morality.
- I was rejecting Judeo-Christian ethics.

In contrast to the emotional and shallow and superficial arguments against drug legalization by the typical drug warrior, the libertarian case for drug freedom is a utilitarian one and a philosophical one and a practical one, but it is also a moral one.

I would like to begin by making two statements—two statements that may not seem radical to most libertarians, but that would not be welcomed in many political and religious circles:

It is neither the job of government nor the business of any individual to prohibit, regulate, restrict, or otherwise control what a man desires to eat, drink, smoke, inject, absorb, snort, sniff, inhale, swallow, or otherwise ingest into his body.

There is no ethical precept in any religion or moral code that should lead anyone to believe that it is the job of government to prohibit, regulate, restrict, or otherwise control what a man desires to eat, drink, smoke, inject, absorb, sniff, inhale, swallow, or otherwise ingest into his body.

I am not saying ...

Now, in making these statements, I want to make clear some things I am not saying.

I am not saying that parents have no right to dictate to their children what is and is not acceptable when it comes to drug use. I just believe that father knows best, not that government knows best. Right now it is a crime in my state of Florida for parents to serve a beer or glass of wine to their children under the age of 21—even if their children are married, have their own children, and serve in the military. That is absurd—and I don't even drink.

I am not saying that employers have no right to mandate that employees abstain from using a particular drug or all drugs, smoking, having a beard, or wearing a pink shirt. Since I believe in freedom and property rights, I believe in the freedom of employers and employees to make employment contracts without government interference. If the owner of a restaurant insists that his waiters wear white tuxedos then they can either visit the local tuxedo shop or look for work elsewhere.

I am not saying that organizations—secular or religious—should not be able to require that their members abstain from drug use—legal or otherwise. Some organizations may mandate the total abstinence of their members from alcohol, drugs, and tobacco. Others might proscribe just alcohol, just drugs, or just tobacco. Still others might merely disdain drunkenness or getting high. Membership in an organization is voluntary, and one man's paradise is another man's prison. In a genuinely free society, restaurants, stores, churches, private clubs, and fraternal organizations would be free to set their own standards and discriminate on the basis of race, gender, sexual orientation, age, political ideology, religious piety, *and drug use.*

I am not saying that there is nothing harmful that can result from something's being eaten, drunk, smoked, injected, absorbed, snorted, sniffed, inhaled, swallowed, or otherwise ingested into one's body. I am well aware of the fact that people die all the time from drug overdoses. However, although people also die from drinking too much alcohol and smoking too many cigarettes, not too many drug prohibitionists ever call for absolute bans on alcohol and tobacco.

I am not saying that anyone should eat, drink, smoke, inject, absorb, snort, sniff, inhale, swallow, or otherwise ingest into his body any drug—legal or illegal. I am not advocating that anyone take any drug—legal or otherwise. The older and more informed I get, the more I am leery of ingesting any drugs, including over-the-counter medications and FDA-approved, physician-prescribed drugs.

I am not saying that I think it is acceptable for anyone to take drugs for any reason other than for medicinal or therapeutic purposes. I consider any other use to be a vice. But as the 19th-century political philosopher Lysander Spooner reminded us, "Vices are not crimes."

I am not saying that I approve of school-bus drivers' smoking a joint while they drive their buses, or mechanics' getting buzzed while they repair your car, or people's walking around stoned in public. Why is it that drug prohibitionists think that all Americans would be on a perpetual high if drugs were legalized? And why is it that they accuse freedom-lovers of desiring or being indifferent to such a society?

I am not saying that individuals and organizations should not be concerned about drug abuse. Most of the negative externalities that result from people's taking drugs are due to the government's war on drugs. In the absence of drug prohibition, drug abuse could be handled the same way as alcohol abuse—by families, friends, churches, rescue missions, Alcoholics Anonymous-type programs, physicians, psychologists, and treatment centers.

The beating heart

All I am saying is that I want the government out of my body. I want the state out of my home, my car, my job, my church, my family, my club, my doctor's office, my insurance company, my bedroom, and my life. All I am saying is that it should be none of anyone's business—as far as the law is concerned—if someone wants to get drunk, high, or stoned in a hotel bar, at a social event, or in his own home. All I am saying is that it is unjust to lock someone up in a cage for smoking a plant. All I am saying is that I want the government to take its hands off drugs and drug paraphernalia, (which are also illegal). Now, I neither use drugs nor own any drug paraphernalia, and I would buy neither even if they were legal, but just the same, I want the government to keep its hands off my property and your property. In the end, it all comes down to property and freedom, as I will argue throughout this essay.

Although evangelical, fundamentalist, independent, and other conservative Christians are some of the first groups that come to mind that zealously back drug prohibition, this is far from a religious issue. The myriad of drug laws in this country—and around the world for that matter—cannot be laid at the feet of conservative Christians. Support for drug prohibition can be found across the political and religious spectrum, encompassing liberals and conservatives, Democrats and Republicans, atheists and theists, the religious and the irreligious. I have heard it said by some libertarians that deep down inside of every man there beats the heart of a libertarian. I disagree. I think rather, and not just on this issue, that there beats the heart of a statist, an authoritarian, and a busybody who wants to remake society in his own image and compel others to live in ways that he approves of. There is no shortage of Americans willing to kill for the military, torture for the CIA, wiretap for the FBI, destroy property for the DEA, and grope for the TSA.

Speaking as a libertarian believer in moral absolutes in general and the ethical principles of the New Testament in particular, I reject federal, state, and local drug prohibition of any kind. I am against drug criminalization, drug regulation, drug restrictions, drug licensing, drug taxing, drug oversight, drug testing, and limiting drugs just to medical use.

Believers in a free society should challenge all laws on drug trafficking, drug manufacturing, drug sales, and drug use. They should object to the 750,000 arrests of Americans every year for marijuana possession. They should protest the incarceration of tens of thousands of Americans for drug-related offenses. They should contest the Harrison Narcotics Tax Act of 1914, the Marijuana Tax Act of 1937, the Comprehensive Drug Abuse Prevention and Control Act of 1970 and its subsequent amendments, the Chemical Diversion and Trafficking Act of 1988, the Illicit Drug Anti-Proliferation Act of 2003, and the Combat Methamphetamine Epidemic Act 2005.

Lovers of liberty should be against the office of the national drug czar, the White House Office of National Drug Control Policy, the National Institute on Drug Abuse, the Narcotics Rewards Program, and the Bureau for International Narcotics and Law Enforcement Affairs.

All freedom-loving Americans should oppose the DEA and its headquarters in Arlington, Virginia, its 21 domestic field divisions, its 227 field offices, its 86 foreign offices in 62 countries, its academy at the Quantico Marine base, its administrator, its deputy administrator, its chief of operations, its chief inspector, its chief financial officer, its chief counsel, its assistant administrators, its 10,000 employees, its 5,500 special agents, its foreign-deployed advisory and support teams, its mobile enforcement teams, its Domestic Cannabis Eradication/Suppression Program (DCE/SP) (which eradicates millions of cultivated outdoor and indoor cannabis plants every year and seizes millions of dollars of cultivator assets), its $2.5 billion budget, and its Office of Aviation Operations with its 106 aircraft and 124 pilots.

I reject the government's war on drugs just as I reject the government's war on poverty, war on cancer, war on terrorism, and war on liquids on airline flights.

I say these things as someone who doesn't use illegal drugs, wouldn't use illicit drugs if they were legalized, and would prefer that no one else use them either. I would remind those who say I am being too extreme that extremism in the defense of liberty is no vice. I guess I could just say that I oppose root and branch every facet of the government's war on drugs, but I want not only to make myself perfectly clear, but also to get people to realize just how broad in scope is the state's war on personal freedom.

Seven reasons

I am choosing my words carefully and deliberately: liberty and freedom, individual liberty and personal freedom. These ideals, along with the sanctity of private property, are fundamental in combating the drug war. That does not mean that there aren't a multitude of other reasons to oppose drug prohibition laws. I can think of seven.

One, the state's war on drugs, like its war on poverty and its war on terrorism, is a failure. It has clogged the judicial system, unnecessarily swelled prison populations, fostered violence, corrupted law enforcement, eroded civil liberties, and destroyed financial privacy. It has encouraged illegal searches and seizures, ruined countless lives, wasted hundreds of billions of taxpayer dollars, hindered legitimate pain treatment, turned law-abiding people into criminals, unreasonably inconvenienced retail shopping, and had no impact on the use or availability of most drugs in the United States. The costs of drug prohibition far outweigh any possible benefits.

Two, drug prohibition is unconstitutional. Conservatives who revere the Constitution should support both the freedom to use drugs for any purpose and a free market in drugs. Nowhere does the Constitution authorize the federal government to intrude itself into the personal eating, drinking, or smoking habits of Americans.

Three, it is not the purpose of government to protect people from bad habits, harmful substances, or vice. As the economist

Ludwig von Mises wrote in *Human Action*,

> Opium and morphine are certainly dangerous, habit-forming drugs. But once the principle is admitted that it is the duty of government to protect the individual against his own foolishness, no serious objections can be advanced against further encroachments.... And why limit the government's benevolent providence to the protection of the individual's body only? Is not the harm a man can inflict on his mind and soul even more disastrous than any bodily evils? Why not prevent him from reading bad books and seeing bad plays, from looking at bad paintings and statues and from hearing bad music? The mischief done by bad ideologies, surely, is much more pernicious, both for the individual and for the whole society, than that done by narcotic drugs.

Four, just as the government has a calculation problem when it comes to central planning of the economy, so also with drug regulation. The government can only arbitrarily decide which drugs should be legal and which drugs shouldn't be, which drugs should be sold to minors and which drugs shouldn't be, which drugs should be regulated and which drugs shouldn't be, whether opium should be classified as Schedule I or Schedule II, and on and on and on. The drug war fosters too much trust in government planners, regulators, and bureaucrats.

Five, there is no government ban on alcohol and tobacco. Yes, they are heavily regulated, but anyone is free to drink and smoke as much as he wants in his own home. Alcohol abuse and heavy tobacco use are two of the leading causes of death in the United States. It seems rather ludicrous to advocate the outlawing of drugs and not the outlawing of alcohol and tobacco.

Six, vices are not crimes. The average American unfortunately equates making the moral case for drug freedom with making the moral case for murder, theft, or arson. But nothing could be further from the truth. In part one, I mentioned Lysander Spooner, and, because I cannot improve on his work, I refer you to the powerful and immortal words at the beginning of his 1875 treatise, *Vices Are Not Crimes*:

Vices are those acts by which a man harms himself or his property.

Crimes are those acts by which one man harms the person or property of another.

Vices are simply the errors which a man makes in his search after his own happiness. Unlike crimes, they imply no malice toward others, and no interference with their persons or property....

Unless this clear distinction between vices and crimes be made and recognized by the laws, there can be on earth no such thing as individual right, liberty, or property; no such things as the right of one man to the control of his own person and property, and the corresponding and co-equal rights of another man to the control of his own person and property.

And seven, it is a grave mistake to look to the state to enforce morality. It is, in fact, quite absurd, since many of the actions of the U.S. government are among the greatest examples of immoral behavior that one could possibly think of. It makes absolutely no sense for the U.S. government to murder millions of Vietnamese, Cambodians, Laotians, Iraqis, and Afghans and then turn around and arrest some poor guy for growing marijuana. Why, then, do so many moral people defend, support, and make excuses for the state, its politicians, its legislation, and its wars? Why would religious people in particular even think of looking to the state to enforce their moral code?

Freedom, always freedom

Practical and utilitarian arguments against the drug war are important, but not as important as the moral argument for the freedom to use or abuse drugs for freedom's sake. The moral case for drug freedom is simply the case for freedom. Freedom to use one's property as one sees fit. Freedom to enjoy the fruits of one's labor in whatever way one deems appropriate. Freedom to use one's body in the manner of one's choosing. Freedom to follow one's own moral code. Freedom from being taxed to fund government tyranny. Freedom from government intrusion into one's personal life. Freedom to be left alone.

It is those of us who advocate the liberty to take drugs and a free market in drugs who are taking the moral high ground. How can anyone with any sense of morality support seizing someone's property, destroying his family, and locking him up in a cage to be raped and humiliated for smoking a plant the government doesn't approve of? What kind of a moral code contains stipulations like that? The case for drug freedom is a moral case because the war on drugs is a war on natural, civil, personal, and constitutional rights. Two wrongs don't make a right. It is not right to act immoral to prevent someone from doing something deemed immoral.

In presenting the moral case for drug freedom I am not distinguishing between legal and illegal drugs or between drugs for medical use and drugs for recreational use. Drugs in and of themselves are not necessarily bad; it depends on how and why they are used. The question is who is going to determine those things. Will it be the individual, in consultation with his family, friends, church, and physician; or will it be the state, in consultation with its legislators, regulators, agents, and bureaucrats? In a free society it is the individual; in an authoritarian society it is the state.

Some libertarians have the idea that absolute drug freedom is a philosophical concept that is fine to intellectually assent to but should never be publicly proclaimed. They consider it an embarrassing, nonessential issue that is best not mentioned outside of libertarian circles. In this regard I like what Mises said:

> [As] soon as we surrender the principle that the state should not interfere in any questions touching on the individual's mode of life, we end by regulating and restricting the latter down to the smallest detail.

There is one mistake, though, that some libertarians have

made. It is one thing to advocate a free society in which individual persons have the liberty to choose a particular lifestyle; but it is inconsistent and ultimately harmful to the cause of liberty to champion a lifestyle choice that considers drug use one of the major tenets of libertarianism, while at the same time championing nonlibertarian issues such as privatizing Social Security, securing educational vouchers, and making taxes fairer.

I am not arguing for the benefits of drugs; I am arguing for the benefits of freedom. Mises again makes a good point:

> A free man must be able to endure it when his fellow men act and live otherwise than he considers proper. He must free himself from the habit, just as soon as something does not please him, of calling for the police.

3

The Case against Medical Marijuana
(Future of Freedom Foundation Commentaries, November 11, 2010)

Pot smokers aren't the only ones disappointed by the rejection of Proposition 19 by California voters. Freedom lovers were just as dissatisfied with the outcome.

Proposition 19, the Regulate, Control & Tax Cannabis Act, would have made it legal for individuals to possess, and authorized retailers to sell to those twenty-one and older, up to one ounce of marijuana.

The ballot initiative lost with almost 54 percent of Californians voting no. This despite arguments that it would generate tax revenue to help with the budget shortfall, reduce crime and violence, cut the profits of drug cartels, ease racial inequities and violations of civil liberties, redirect law enforcement resources, and lower law-enforcement and incarceration costs.

Both the California Republican and Democratic candidates for U.S. senator and governor in the recent election opposed Proposition 19 even though many California county Democratic Parties supported the measure.

I suspect, however, that most of the same people that voted down Proposition 19 would go ballistic if the state of California outlawed alcohol and smoking even though alcohol abuse and tobacco smoking use are two of the leading causes of death in the United States.

The defeat of Proposition 19 does not mean that no one in California can legally smoke pot. California, like fourteen other states, has legalized the medical use of marijuana, albeit with certain restrictions. According to the California Health and Safety Code: "Seriously ill Californians have the right to obtain and use marijuana for medical purposes where that medical use is deemed appropriate and has been recommended by a physician who has determined that the person's health would benefit from the use of marijuana."

Still, marijuana use for any purpose remains illegal according to federal law—as it has been since 1937. In fact, the defendant in the *Gonzales v. Raich* (2005) case that confirmed the power of the federal government under the Constitution's commerce clause to ban the medical use of marijuana was Angel Raich of California.

The statist case against legalizing marijuana, whether uttered by liberals or conservatives, is that marijuana is a gateway drug, overall drug use would increase, the wrong message would be sent to young people, pot smoking is immoral, and marijuana is much more potent today than it was a generation ago.

If you dare to call for the full legalization of all drugs, then you are just dismissed as a crackpot because what you are advocating is, as former drug czar Bill "I lost millions in Vegas" Bennett said, "stupid and morally atrocious."

Some statists are incorrigible, and reject even the medical use of marijuana because pot smoking is immoral no matter what the purpose, people will just lie about their medical need in order to get the drug, marijuana is just too dangerous a substance to sanction its use for any reason, and, of course, because everyone knows there are no real medical benefits to smoking marijuana.

But many who reject sane and logical arguments—like some studies have found that smoking marijuana is less dangerous than drinking alcohol and the costs of drug prohibition far outweigh the benefits—are nevertheless willing to make a medical exception when it comes to marijuana for those who are seriously or terminally ill.

They recognize that the smoking of marijuana is thought to provide medical benefits for Alzheimer's disease, Parkinson's disease, cancer, muscle spasms, pain, loss of appetite, muscle spasms, stomach cramps, nausea, multiple sclerosis, inflammation, epilepsy, AIDS / HIV, cachexia, and glaucoma.

How nice, how compassionate, and how benevolent are

those who are willing to make a medical exception to their aversion to marijuana legalization—and how wrong.

How tyrannical it is that in America—where thousands of people every year have elective or plastic surgery—governments prevent people from using marijuana except for medical reasons. How cruel it is that in America—"land of the free"—people have to suffer with some sickness because they don't meet some arbitrary requirement to obtain the medication they want. How authoritarian it is that in America—"sweet land of liberty" —people need to have a government-issued medical card before they can purchase certain medications. How dictatorial it is that in America—with its Bill of Rights—people can only have a government-approved medical treatment. How repressive it is that in America—"where at least I know I'm free"—people cannot have access to medication without first paying to see a doctor.

The paternalistic, nanny, regulatory state is at its worse when it comes to the war on drugs. As C.S. Lewis remarked:

> Of all tyrannies a tyranny sincerely exercised for the good of its victims may be the most oppressive. It may be better to live under robber barons than under omnipotent moral busybodies. The robber baron's cruelty may sometimes sleep, his cupidity may at some point be satiated; but those who torment us for our own good will torment us without end for they do so with the approval of their own conscience.

How hypocritical it is that in America—"God bless the USA"—the government demonizes marijuana even though millions of people get lung cancer from smoking cigarettes and cirrhosis of the liver from drinking alcohol. The sin taxes on these substances mean that the government needs people to use them even while discouraging their use. This is especially true in the case of cigarettes, whose advertising on television and radio has been banned since 1971. And although alcohol is a factor in many car accidents, boating accidents, and child abuse cases, there are nine states where it is the state government that operates the liquor stores.

How tragic it is that in America—with its caring liberals and compassionate conservatives—the majority of the American people fully support their government's restrictions on the use of marijuana.

The libertarian case against medical marijuana is straightforward. There should be no laws regarding the buying, selling, growing, use, processing, or possession of marijuana for medical reasons. This is because there should be no laws of any kind regarding the medicinal, therapeutic, or recreational use of marijuana. And that's not all. The only honest and consistent libertarian position is that there should be no laws regarding the buying, selling, growing, processing, use, or possession of any drug for any reason.

"The only freedom which deserves the name," said John Stuart Mill,

> is that of pursuing our own good in our own way, so long as we do not attempt to deprive others of theirs, or impede their efforts to obtain it. Each is the proper guardian of his own health, whether bodily, or mental and spiritual. Mankind are greater gainers by suffering each other to live as seems good to themselves, than by compelling each to live as seems good to the rest.

Pot prohibition is the cornerstone of a police state. No country can be described as a free society when its government demonizes a plant and arrests over 750,000 of its citizens a year for possessing it.

4

Why Don't Conservatives Oppose the War on Drugs?
(Future of Freedom Foundation Commentaries, November 24, 2010)

The war on drugs is a failure.

According to the latest National Survey on Drug Use and Health conducted by the Substance Abuse and Mental Health Services Administration: "Drug use in the United States increased in 2009, reversing downward trends since 2002. " There was a spike in the number of Americans admitting to using marijuana, ecstasy, and methamphetamine.

Yet, no matter how much it costs to wage the drug war (more than $41 billion according to a just-released Cato Institute study), conservatives generally support it. I know of no prominent conservative who publicly calls for drug legalization. I know of no Republican candidate in the recent election (outside of Ron Paul) who has ever publicly voiced his support for the decriminalization of drug possession. Republicans in Congress—by an overwhelming majority—have even criminalized the purchase of over-the-counter allergy-relief products like Sudafed because they contain pseudoephedrine.

Negative arguments about how the war on drugs ruins lives, erodes civil liberties, and destroys financial privacy are unpersuasive to most conservatives. None of these things matter to the typical conservative because they, like most Americans of any political persuasion, see using drugs for recreational use as immoral.

The hypocrisy of conservatives who support the war on drugs but not the prohibition of alcohol should be readily apparent. But aside from a small minority of conservative religious people that long for the days of Prohibition, conservatives generally don't support making the drinking of alcohol a crime even though alcohol is a factor in many accidents, crimes, and premature deaths. So why is getting high on drugs treated differently from getting high on alcohol?

The reason conservatives should oppose the war on drugs is a simple one that has nothing to do with positive, negative, or financial arguments. Drug prohibition by the federal government is simply unconstitutional. Conservatives claim to revere the Constitution. They regularly lambaste judges for being activists and not strict constitutionalists. In the "Pledge to America" they released a few weeks before the recent election, House Republicans promised to "honor the Constitution as constructed by its framers and honor the original intent of those precepts that have been consistently ignored—particularly the Tenth Amendment."

In article I, section 8, of the Constitution, there are eighteen specific powers granted to Congress. We call these the enumerated powers. Everything else is reserved to the states—with or without the Tenth Amendment. Nowhere does the Constitution authorize the federal government to concern itself with the nature and quantity of any substance Americans inhale or otherwise take into their body. Nowhere does the Constitution authorize the federal government to prohibit drug manufacture, sale, or use. Nowhere does the Constitution authorize the federal government to ban anything. When the Progressives wanted the United States government to ban alcohol, they realized that an amendment to the Constitution was needed.

Drug prohibition is likewise incompatible with private property, individual liberty, personal responsibility, free markets, and limited government—things that conservatives claim to believe in. What happened to the conservative emphasis on families, churches, private charities, and faith-based organizations solving problems instead of looking to the federal government to solve them?

But if conservatives want a war on drugs or any other personal freedom, then from a constitutional standpoint it is at the state level that they must wage their war. From a libertarian standpoint, state (or local) attempts to prohibit or to tax and/or regulate drugs are likewise attacks on property and freedom. But from a constitutional perspective, conservatives should be just as against a federal war on drugs as libertarians are.

So, if conservatives want to be both constitutional and consistent, they would have to say that there should be no National Drug Control Strategy, no National Survey on Drug Use and Health, and no Domestic Cannabis Eradication/Suppression Program. They would have to say that the Substance Abuse and Mental Health Services Administration, the Office of National Drug Control Policy, and the Drug Enforcement Administration should all be abolished. And they would have to say that the Controlled Substances Act, Comprehensive Drug Abuse Prevention and Control Act, and Combat Methamphetamine Epidemic Act should all be repealed.

Although I would vehemently oppose their war on drugs at the state and local level, conservatives could abolish all those federal agencies while at the same time waging a relentless war on drugs—and all vice—at the state and local levels.

Why do conservatives, who profess to revere individual liberty, free markets, private property, limited government, and the Constitution continue to support the war on drugs?

5

Drug-Warrior Hypocrisy

(*Future of Freedom Foundation Commentaries*, December 3, 2010)

Statists of every variety—left/right, liberal/conservative, Democrat/Republican, progressive/moderate—disagree vocally and often. Although these groups may argue among themselves and with each other about any number of issues—health care, education, Social Security, the environment, tax cuts, business regulations—they all have one thing in common. The statists are all paternalistic and believe in some kind of a nanny state to monitor the behavior of its citizens.

Oh, statists may disagree on the nature, scope, and features of their vision of the nanny state, but rarely on its necessity.

This paternalism is at its worse when it comes to the war on drugs. It is here where caring liberals and compassionate conservatives unite with the religious and the irreligious to not only deprive people of their natural, moral, civil, and constitutional rights to buy, sell, grow, manufacture, or ingest *whatever* substance they choose for *whatever* reason they choose, but to criminalize such activity, and sometimes severely.

This attitude of prohibition and criminalization is ultimately based on two things: taking drugs is bad for one's health and taking drugs is morally corrupting.

The hypocrisy of drug warriors is legion.

Every bad thing that could be said regarding drug abuse could also be said of alcohol abuse—and even more so.

Alcohol abuse is a factor in many drownings, home accidents, suicides, pedestrian accidents, fires, car accidents, violent crimes, boating accidents, child abuse cases, sex crimes, and divorces. The number one killer of young people under twenty-five is alcohol-related automobile accidents.

22

Alcohol abuse is one of the leading causes of premature deaths in the United States. It can also be a contributing factor in cases of cancer, mental illness, and cirrhosis of the liver. And obviously, it is the cause of various fetal alcohol spectrum disorders.

According to a study by the Independent Scientific Committee on Drugs recently published in the prestigious medical journal *The Lancet*, alcohol ranks as the "most harmful drug," beating out heroin, crack cocaine, and ecstasy. Numerous studies have shown that smoking marijuana is much safer than drinking alcohol.

Yet, in spite of the negative effects of alcohol on morals and health, few Americans would like to return to the days of Prohibition.

But it's not just on the subject of alcohol that the hypocrisy of drug warriors is manifest.

People from all across the political spectrum generally resent federal, state, and local government efforts to regulate what they eat and drink.

The San Francisco Board of Supervisors recently voted to forbid restaurants from giving gifts with meals (like McDonald's Happy Meals) that contain too much fat and sugar. Some cities have banned the use of trans fats in food preparation. Bacon-wrapped hot dogs were banned in Los Angeles in 2008. A bill introduced in the New York legislature earlier this year would have banned the use of salt in restaurant cooking. Ten states ban the sale of unpasteurized raw milk. Officials with the county Office for the Aging in Putnam County, New York, prohibited the donation to senior citizen centers of unused cakes, donuts, and pastries from local bakeries because it set a bad nutritional precedent. Many school districts have banned soft drinks and junk food from school cafeterias. Some politicians have even called for warning labels or taxes on junk food. The Food and Drug Administration has its food pyramid that promotes grains and demonizes fat—something that more and more doctors and nutritionists are coming to realize is the cause rather than the cure for heart disease, diabetes, and obesity.

Civil libertarians, freedom lovers, and strict constitutionalists decry—and rightly so—many, if not all, of these nanny-state
measures to control what people consume. But most of these
same people are ardent drug warriors who have no problem
locking up their fellow Americans in a cage for consuming a
substance that the government doesn't approve of.
The fact that most U.S. prisons are overcrowded with
non-violent drug offenders, that waging the war on drugs costs
American taxpayers over $40 billion a year, and that the costs of
drug prohibition far outweigh the benefits is of no consequence
to these health and morals crusaders.

But the hypocrisy of drug warriors is not their only short-
coming. Even worse is their failure to see the dangerous result
of their acquiescing to the state, as this classic passage from the
Austrian economist Ludwig von Mises so eloquently explains:

> Opium and morphine are certainly dangerous, habit-forming
> drugs. But once the principle is admitted that it is the duty
> of government to protect the individual against his own
> foolishness, no serious objections can be advanced against
> further encroachments. A good case could be made out in
> favor of the prohibition of alcohol and nicotine. And why
> limit the government's benevolent providence to the protec-
> tion of the individual's body only? Is not the harm a man
> can inflict on his mind and soul even more disastrous than
> any bodily evils? Why not prevent him from reading bad
> books and seeing bad plays, from looking at bad paintings
> and statues and from hearing bad music? The mischief done
> by bad ideologies, surely, is much more pernicious, both for
> the individual and for the whole society, than that done by
> narcotic drugs.
>
> These fears are not merely imaginary specters terrifying
> secluded doctrinaires. It is a fact that no paternal govern-
> ment, whether ancient or modern, ever shrank from regi-
> menting its subjects' minds, beliefs, and opinions. If one
> abolishes man's freedom to determine his own consumption,
> one takes all freedoms away. The naive advocates of govern-
> ment interference with consumption delude themselves

when they neglect what they disdainfully call the philosophical aspect of the problem. They unwittingly support the case of censorship, inquisition, religious intolerance, and the persecution of dissenters.

Drug warriors can't have it both ways. No free society is worthy of the name if its government can selectively ban certain drugs. Any prohibition on the manufacture, sale, possession, or medicinal, therapeutic, or recreational use of drugs is an attack on personal freedom. The war on drugs is a war on liberty. A moral and healthy society achieved at the cost of liberty is not worth having.

6

The Drug War Is Expanding
(Future of Freedom Foundation Commentaries, February 8, 2011)*

There is no question that the war on drugs is a failure. In spite of decades of prohibition laws, threats of fines and/or imprisonments, and massive propaganda campaigns, drugs are available and affordable. The Mental Health Services Administration—a government agency—has reported that marijuana, ecstasy, and methamphetamine use has recently increased. The government's GAO has even said that the D.A.R.E. program has had "no statistically significant long-term effect on preventing youth illicit drug use."

There are, however, some things that the war on drugs has accomplished. It has drained $40 billion a year from government treasuries. It has made criminals out of hundreds of thousands of Americans (754,224 Americans were arrested for marijuana possession in 2008). It has destroyed financial privacy. It has unnecessarily swelled prison populations (over half of the federal prison population is because of drug charges). It has turned America's inner cities into war zones. It has greatly eroded civil liberties. It has corrupted law enforcement. It has ruined more lives than drugs themselves.

The war on drugs enjoys wide bipartisan support on both the federal and state levels. Sure, some states have relaxed marijuana laws and made marijuana legal for medical use, but always under the watchful eye of state regulators and tax authorities.

But in these days of budget crises, on both the federal and state levels, the war on drugs is expanding. The latest addition to the list of controlled substances will be bath salts.

White House drug czar Gil Kerlikowske has issued a bath salt alarm because the synthetic stimulants mephedrone and methylenedioxypyrovalerone (MDPV) are being sold as bath salts. It turns out that instead of using these bath salts in the bathtub, people have taken to swallowing, snorting, injecting, smoking, and otherwise ingesting them.

Senator Charles Schumer (D-NY) plans to introduce legislation to ban these drugs disguised as bath salts as federally controlled substances. "The longer we wait to ban the substances, the greater risk we put our kids in," said Schumer.

Several states have already banned or are considering legislation to ban the dreaded bath salts. In my state of Florida, the attorney general, Pam Bondi, has banned them for ninety days of her own accord because the Florida attorney general has the power to temporarily ban a substance if it is found to be an immediate threat to consumers. It will now be a third degree felony to sell products containing MDVP. According to Bondi, energized bath salt is "right up there with cocaine and heroin." She claims that MDVP makes you "think you're seeing monsters and it also makes you think that you can fly, and there are a lot of balconies out there for spring break." Health effects supposedly include increased heart rate, nosebleeds, hallucinations, severe paranoia, seizures, and kidney failure. Florida Senate president Mike Haridopolis says that Florida legislators would work to ban the substance this spring. That is a mouthful coming from a man who claims he "has stood up for Floridians against more government."

The issue here is not how high one might get from the use of these bath salts, how many monsters one might see, how many ways a person might damage his health, how easy it might be to purchase the bath salts, how cheap it might be to infuse the bath salts with the stimulants, how many spring breakers in Florida might jump off hotel balconies, or even if one sniff of bath salts might kill you.

The case against the banning or regulating of narcotic bath salts is the same as the case against banning or regulating marijuana, crack cocaine, or crystal meth.

First of all, the federal government has no constitutional authority to ban or regulate drugs. Drug warriors may wish that it did, but no amount of wishing, desiring, or wanting the federal government to have that power can override the Constitution.

Two, government in general should not have the authority, constitutional or otherwise, to ban or regulate drugs. Period. The reason for the government intervention, whether it be for public health, child safety, moral sensibilities, or community standards, is irrelevant. It is just not the business of government to intervene in this fashion.

Three, to be consistent, government at all levels should, and drug warriors should support, the banning of alcohol and tobacco since they are two of the leading causes of death in the United States. It is the height of hypocrisy to call for drug prohibition and not the prohibition of other harmful substances.

Four, recreational drugs are far less likely to kill you than physician-prescribed drugs. According to some articles in the *Journal of the American Medical Association*, over 100,000 people die every year from drugs prescribed and administered by physicians. Over two million Americans a year have in-hospital adverse drug reactions. The war on drugs is completely misdirected.

Five, drug prohibition and regulation are incompatible with private property, individual liberty, personal responsibility, and free markets. Indeed, drug prohibition and regulation are anathema to a free society. The war on drugs is a war on liberty.

The libertarian case for drug freedom is consistently straightforward: There should be no laws at any level of government for any reason regarding the buying, selling, growing, processing, manufacturing, advertising, use, or possession of any drug for any reason.

This does not mean that libertarians advocate the use of hallucinogenic drugs. This does not mean that libertarians don't think that employers could require that their employees not use drugs. This does not mean that libertarians don't think that parents have the right to forbid their children from using drugs. This does not mean that libertarians don't think that using drugs could be harmful to one's health. This does not mean that libertarians don't think that getting stoned is immoral. This does not mean that libertarians don't care if someone has a drug problem.

The real issue is not even about drugs.

It is just not the business of government to ban or regulate what someone decides to put into his mouth, nose, or veins. It doesn't matter if it's immoral, unhealthy, sinful, hazardous, stupid, disgusting, or death inducing. The legislators and bureaucrats who make the decisions to ban or not to ban and to regulate or not to regulate are not parents, nannies, doctors, priests, psychologists, guards, monitors, or gods—or are they?

Once you elevate government to such a level that you allow it to determine what you can and can't ingest or regulate the circumstances under which you can lawfully ingest something, there is no stopping its reach, as Ludwig von Mises explained over fifty years ago:

> If it is true that government derives its authority from God and is entrusted by Providence to act as the guardian of the ignorant and stupid populace, then it is certainly its task to regiment every aspect of the subject's conduct. The God-sent ruler knows better what is good for his wards than they do themselves. It is his duty to guard them against the harm they would inflict upon themselves if left alone.

Although the war on drugs doesn't need to be expanded, it likewise doesn't need to be scaled back, made more consistent, made more effective, or made more efficient. For the sake of freedom, it needs to be ended—completely, quickly, and permanently.

7

Baseball, Steroids, and a Free Society
(Future of Freedom Foundation Commentaries, April 11, 2011)

Even non-baseball fans like me couldn't help but notice that right in the middle of Barry Bonds' perjury trial Manny Ramirez abruptly retired rather than face a 100-game suspension for violating Major League Baseball's drug policy—for the second time.

Former Pittsburgh Pirates and San Francisco Giants outfielder and fourteen-time All-Star Bonds was charged with three counts of making false statements to a grand jury and one count of obstruction of justice. Although he was indicted in 2007, his trial did not begin until recently, on March 21, 2011. Bonds' legal troubles stem from his 2003 grand-jury testimony in a scandal involving the supplying of steroids to athletes. Bonds allegedly lied under oath about his alleged use of steroids. On April 13, after the federal government spent tens of millions of dollars, Bonds was found guilty of obstructing justice, but the jury failed to reach a verdict on the other counts.

Tampa Bay Rays slugger Ramirez faced a 100-game suspension after testing positive for a performance-enhancing drug during spring training. He previously served a 50-game suspension for violating the League's drug policy in 2009 while he was playing with the Los Angeles Dodgers. The penalty for a second violation is double the first penalty.

Major League Baseball has prohibited the possession, sale, or use of illegal drugs and controlled substances since 1991. Formal drug testing was instituted in 2004. Twelve players on major-league rosters were suspended for ten days each in 2005 after testing positive for prohibited substances. Under tougher rules in force because of the new Joint Drug Prevention and Treatment Program in 2006, three players received a fifty-game suspension. Seven players received a variety of suspensions in 2007. One player in 2008 and two players in 2009 and 2010 received fifty-game suspensions.

An all-day, nationally televised congressional hearing was held by the House Government Reform Committee on March 17, 2005, on steroid use in baseball and Major League Baseball's drug policy. Said Rep. Henry Waxman (D–CA) in an interview a few days before the hearing: "Kids are dying from the use of steroids. They're looking up to these major-league leaders in terms of the enhancements that they're using. And we have to stop it."

In 2006, after pressure from several influential members of Congress, former U.S. Senator George Mitchell was appointed by Commissioner of Baseball Bud Selig to investigate drug use in baseball. On December 13, 2007, Mitchell issued his 409-page *Report to the Commissioner of Baseball of an Independent Investigation into the Illegal Use of Steroids and Other Performance Enhancing Substances by Players in Major League Baseball* (The Mitchell Report). The report named eighty-nine baseball players who allegedly used illegal performance- enhancing drugs.

On January 15, 2008, the same House committee as in 2005, but now called the House Committee on Oversight and Government Reform, held another hearing to discuss the findings in the Mitchell Report and assess Major League Baseball's progress in combating the use of performance-enhancing drugs by its players. Another hearing was held on February 13.

Statists on the left and the right generally support both Major League Baseball's drug policy and the federal war on drugs. Libertarians, however, are ambivalent on the former and oppose the latter.

The federal war on drugs is undefendable. Not only has it failed to curtail drug use, it has eroded civil liberties, destroyed financial privacy, corrupted law enforcement, crowded prisons with non-violent offenders, ruined countless lives, and wasted hundreds of billions of taxpayer dollars.

Nowhere does the Constitution grant the federal government the power to prohibit, regulate, restrict, control, license,

monitor, or otherwise concern itself with any substance
—including those deemed harmful or mood-altering—that any
American—including professional athletes and other role
models—desires to inject, swallow, sniff or otherwise ingest into
his body. This means that congressional committees to investigate drug use are, like the war on drugs itself, in violation of the
Constitution.

It doesn't matter how potent or how harmful a particular
drug might be. It doesn't matter if it is immoral to get high or
use steroids. It doesn't matter—however tragic it might be—that
you had a family member or friend who died from a drug
overdose. It doesn't matter if using drugs is a vice or a sin. It still
doesn't change the fact that the federal government has no
authority to ban any substance or intrude into the personal lives
of Americans.

Libertarians don't stop with the Constitution, of course.
The war on drugs is a war on individual liberty, personal
responsibility, private property, limited government, and a free
society.

This doesn't mean that libertarians support drug use,
condone drug use, or encourage drug use. This doesn't mean
that libertarians don't recognize the potentially harmful effects
of ingesting drugs—legal or illegal, mood-altering or performance-enhancing, prescription or over-the-counter, medicinal
or therapeutic. It simply means that we believe in a free society
and the proper role of government. It is families, friends,
counselors, and churches that should be advising individuals on
the decision to use or not to use drugs, and it is physicians,
psychologists, and drug treatment centers that should be dealing
with the problems of drug abuse—not some paternalistic nanny
state.

But none of this means that libertarians think baseball
players should have the absolute right to choose to use steroids,
human-growth hormones, supplements, or other performance-
enhancing drugs independently of their employers' rules and
regulations. Major League Baseball—and any other private
organization—should have the freedom to set or not to set its

own drug-use policies. In the case of baseball, this might range from a policy of actually supplying to players performance-enhancing drugs of various kinds to a draconian zero-tolerance policy that bans permanently from baseball any player caught using any drug deemed off-limits by the baseball commissioner to the much more likely scenario of something in between.

In a free society, Major League Baseball would make its own drug policy with or without input from the team owners, the fans, the players, or the players' union. The government wouldn't be involved in any way. Team owners who didn't like the policy could lobby and cooperate to change it or form their own league. Fans that didn't like it could stay home from the ballpark. Players that didn't like it could quit. If the players' union didn't like it, then it could try to persuade the players to strike. Drug policy could also be left up to each individual team. But again, the government wouldn't be involved in any way.

There are other misconceptions about the libertarian case for drug freedom as well. In a libertarian society; that is, a free society, drugs would be legal but employers would have the right to prohibit specific drugs or all drugs from being in the pockets, lockers, and bodies of their employees. Employee drug testing might be scheduled, random, or non-existent. This is because any property owner would have the right to control what takes place on his property as he sees fit, including prescribing, proscribing, or permitting whatever persons or substances he chooses without the government being involved in any way.

8

U.S. Attorneys Crack down on the Tenth Amendment
(Future of Freedom Foundation Commentaries, May 4, 2011)

Since just last month, the Arizona Department of Health Services has been accepting applications for medical marijuana patient and caregiver cards. Voters in Arizona approved an initiative placed on the ballot via a citizen petition, Proposition 203, the "Arizona Medical Marijuana Act," in the general election last November. The measure, which took effect on April 14, narrowly passed by a vote of 841,346 to 837,005. So, despite opposition to Proposition 203 from all of Arizona's sheriffs and county prosecutors, the governor, and the state attorney general, medical marijuana is now legal in Arizona.

Fourteen other states besides Arizona (Alaska, California, Colorado, Hawaii, Maine, Michigan, Montana, Nevada, New Jersey, New Mexico, Oregon, Rhode Island, Vermont, and Washington) have already legalized marijuana for medical use. Medical cannabis is also legal in the District of Columbia.

Once their application is approved and their registry card is issued, Arizonans can buy, possess, and use up to 2.5 ounces of marijuana every two weeks. They can also grow up to 12 marijuana plants if they don't live within 25 miles of a medical marijuana dispensary.

But because the state of Arizona, like the federal government and the other forty-nine states, doesn't believe in giving its citizens complete freedom to do "anything that's peaceful," there are numerous restrictions and certain rules that must be followed. Lighting up in public places or at dispensaries is illegal. Pot plants can't be planted openly in one's backyard; they can only be grown in an enclosed, locked facility. Marijuana cannot be given to anyone without a valid registry card. And no one can apply for a card without written certification from a licensed

Arizona physician stating that he has one of the "debilitating conditions" recognized by the state (AIDS, cancer, glaucoma, hepatitis C, "severe and chronic pain," etc.).

Applying for a patient or caregiver card is not exactly easy either. There is a fee of $150 for a patient card ($75 if one is on food stamps) and $200 for a caregiver card (for those who purchase marijuana on behalf of a sick patient). A criminal record check must be passed (convicted felons need not apply), and fingerprints must be submitted. Everything must be submitted online using the proper forms in PDF format. Cards are only valid for a year, and renewal fees are the same as the initial fees.

States legalizing limited amounts of marijuana for medical use or decriminalizing limited amounts of marijuana for recreational use, which some states and cities have also done, is certainly a step in a libertarian direction; that is, a step toward more freedom and less government control over peaceful activity. But as I have pointed out elsewhere, there should be no laws regarding the buying, selling, growing, using, processing, or possessing of marijuana—or any other drug—for any reason, medical or otherwise.

But even this small step taken by Arizona toward individual liberty and personal responsibility is in jeopardy by the federal government. Permitting the use of marijuana—for any reason—actually conflicts with federal laws against the cultivation, sale, or use of marijuana that have been in place since 1937. The power of the federal government to override state and local laws that allow cannabis was confirmed by the U.S. Supreme Court in *Gonzales v. Raich* (2005).

On October 19, 2009, Deputy Attorney General David Ogden issued to U.S. attorneys a "Memorandum for Selected United State Attorneys on Investigations and Prosecutions in States Authorizing the Medical Use of Marijuana." This document reads in part:

> The prosecution of significant traffickers of illegal drugs, including marijuana, and the disruption of illegal drug manufacturing and trafficking networks continues to be a core priority in the department's efforts against narcotics

and dangerous drugs, and the department's investigative and prosecutorial resources should be directed towards these objectives. As a general matter, pursuit of these priorities should not focus federal resources in your States on individuals whose actions are in clear and unambiguous compliance with existing state laws providing for the medical use of marijuana. For example, prosecution of individuals with cancer or other serious illnesses who use marijuana as part of a recommended treatment regimen consistent with applicable state law, or those caregivers in clear and unambiguous compliance with existing state law who provide such individuals with marijuana, is unlikely to be an efficient use of limited federal resources.

In announcing these guidelines, Attorney General Eric Holder said:

It will not be a priority to use federal resources to prosecute patients with serious illnesses or their caregivers who are complying with state laws on medical marijuana, but we will not tolerate drug traffickers who hide behind claims of compliance with state law to mask activities that are clearly illegal. This balanced policy formalizes a sensible approach that the department has been following since January: effectively focus our resources on serious drug traffickers while taking into account state and local laws.

According to a story in the *Arizona Republic*, U.S. attorneys in California and Washington have recently told officials in those states that they intend to enforce federal laws that prohibit manufacture and distribution of marijuana:

U.S. attorneys in Washington state say a bill expected to reach the desk of Gov. Chris Gregoire this weekend could open landlords, dispensary owners and even state employees to prosecution under federal drug laws.

A U.S. attorney in California made similar comments about a city law in Oakland allowing marijuana warehouses.

This has been perplexing to state employees and potential

dispensary owners in Arizona, and with good reason. A letter from the U.S. attorney for the Northern District of California to the Oakland city attorney makes it clear that the federal government views "growing, distributing, and possessing marijuana in any capacity, other than as part of a federally authorized research program," as "a violation of federal law regardless of state laws permitting such activities":

> The department is concerned about the Oakland ordinance's creation of a licensing scheme that permits large-scale industrial marijuana cultivation and manufacturing as it authorizes conduct contrary to federal law and threatens the federal government's efforts to regulate the possession, manufacturing, and trafficking of controlled substances. Accordingly, the department is carefully considering civil and criminal legal remedies regarding those who seek to set up industrial marijuana growing warehouses in Oakland pursuant to licenses issued by the City of Oakland, individuals who elect to operate "industrial cannabis cultivation and manufacturing facilities" will be doing so in violation of federal law. Others who knowingly facilitate the actions of the licensees, including property owners, landlords, and financiers should also know that their conduct violates federal law. Potential actions the department is considering include injunctive actions to prevent cultivation and distribution of marijuana and other associated violations of the CSA; civil fines; criminal prosecution; and the forfeiture of any property used to facilitate a violation of the CSA.

Federal agents have already raided marijuana dispensaries in Montana, Michigan, and California.

In cracking down on those who grow, distribute, and use marijuana, U.S. attorneys are actually cracking down on the Tenth Amendment to the Constitution. The Tenth Amendment reinforces the truth that the power of Congress is limited to what is specifically enumerated in Article I, Section 8, of the Constitution. It makes it clear that "the powers not delegated to the United States by the Constitution, nor prohibited by it to the States, are reserved to the States respectively, or to the people."

Congress has been granted no power to ban, regulate, or otherwise interfere with the production, sale, distribution, possession, or use of marijuana for the simple reason that it has no authority over any drug. Congress has no constitutional right to label anything a controlled substance.

The argument of the majority in *Gonzales v. Raich* (2005) that Congress has the power under the commerce clause to criminalize the production and use marijuana, even where states have approved its medical, use was answered in a blistering dissent by Justice Clarence Thomas:

> By holding that Congress may regulate activity that is neither interstate nor commerce under the Interstate Commerce Clause, the Court abandons any attempt to enforce the Constitution's limits on federal power.

> Certainly no evidence from the founding suggests that "commerce" included the mere possession of a good or some purely personal activity that did not involve trade or exchange for value. In the early days of the republic, it would have been unthinkable that Congress could prohibit the local cultivation, possession, and consumption of marijuana.

> If the federal government can regulate growing a half-dozen cannabis plants for personal consumption (not because it is interstate commerce, but because it is inextricably bound up with interstate commerce), then Congress' Article I powers —as expanded by the necessary and proper clause—have no meaningful limits.

> Congress has encroached on states' traditional police powers to define the criminal law and to protect the health, safety, and welfare of their citizens.

> If the majority is to be taken seriously, the federal government may now regulate quilting bees, clothes drives, and potluck suppers throughout the 50 States. This makes a mockery of Madison's assurance to the people of New York that the "powers delegated" to the federal government are

"few and defined," while those of the States are "numerous and indefinite."

The crackdown on marijuana by U.S. attorneys is an attack on the Constitution, the Founding Fathers, the principle of federalism, and the very nature of our republic. Although an ABC news poll taken last year showed that 81 percent of Americans were in favor of legalizing marijuana for medical use, this has nothing to do with why the federal war on marijuana should be ended. It all comes down to the issue of the legitimate powers of the federal government, not anyone's preference for or against marijuana.

Conservative drug warriors—if they really revere the Constitution like they claim they do—are going to have to change their approach. In the country of Singapore, the penalty is capital punishment for possession of more than 15 grams of cannabis. Many "drug traffickers" have been hung in Singapore. This came up once on a segment of the *O'Reilly Factor*. When Bill O'Reilly interviewed Newt Gingrich, here is part of the exchange that took place:

> Now, they have no drug problem in Singapore at all, number one, because they hang drug dealers—they execute them. And number two, the market is very thin, because when they catch you using, you go away with a mandatory rehab. You go to some rehab center, which they have, which the government has built. The United States does not have the stomach for that. We don't have the stomach for that, Mr. Speaker.

> Well, I think it's time we get the stomach for that, Bill. And I think we need a program—I would dramatically expand testing. I think we have—and I agree with you. I would try to use rehabilitation. I'd make it mandatory. And I think we have every right as a country to demand of our citizens that they quit doing illegal things which are funding, both in Afghanistan and in Mexico and in Colombia, people who are destroying civilization.

The same goes even for those diehard-Republican, red-state, ultra-conservative drug-warrior prohibitionists who go beyond O'Reilly and Gingrich. Any laws regarding the production, sale, distribution, possession, or use of marijuana—whether we agree with them or not—need to be passed at the state level. So, whether someone wants the death penalty for drug dealers and drug users or just fines and mandatory treatment, it is at the state level that these things must be decided instead of a one-size-fits all dictate handed down from Washington.

Libertarians would, of course, vehemently oppose even state and local wars on marijuana and other drugs, but at least these don't make a mockery of the Constitution and our federal system of government.

9

Why Is the U.S. Fighting Mexico's Drug War?
(Future of Freedom Foundation Commentaries, May 25, 2011)

In December of 2006, Mexico's new president, Felipe Calderón, declared war on drug cartels. "We need to win. And we will win. That's my idea. I'm sure about that," he said in an "ABC News" interview. But winning this war is coming at a heavy price: assassinations of government officials, horrific gun battles in Mexican streets, kidnappings, thousands dead, and the loss of trade, investment, and tourism.

The Mexican government deployed over 40,000 military troops last year dedicated to counter-narcotics activities in assistance of civilian law-enforcement authorities.

In order to draw a distinction between casual users and drug traffickers, in August of 2009 Mexico enacted a "personal use" law that decriminalized the possession of small amounts of marijuana (5 g), cocaine (.5 g), heroin (50 mg), and other drugs including LSD (.015 mg) and methamphetamine (40 mg). "This is not legalization," said Bernardo Espino del Castillo of the attorney general's office, it is "regulating the issue and giving citizens greater legal certainty." Anyone caught with amounts under the legal limits will be encouraged to seek treatment. Treatment is mandatory for third-time offenders. At the same time, though, penalties have been toughened for drug dealers. Although the new law hasn't changed things much, I suppose it has kept some non-violent addicts out of jail.

The former president of Mexico, Vicente Fox, favors a different approach: legalization. Fox said that fear and violence is destroying Mexican society and that Mexico is losing young lives at an alarming rate as a result of the drug war. He looks to Portugal, which decriminalized all drugs ten years ago, as a model for a solution.

Regardless of how the government of Mexico decides to wage the war on drugs, one thing is for certain: the U.S. government should not be fighting Mexico's drug war. But that is exactly what our government is doing.

An undisclosed numbers of U.S. law-enforcement agents work in Mexico. What we do know, thanks to an Associated Press investigation, is that the U.S. law-enforcement role in Mexico has surged. The DEA has more than 60 agents in Mexico. There are in addition 40 Immigration and Customs Enforcement agents, 20 Marshal Service deputies, and 18 Alcohol, Tobacco, Firearms and Explosives agents, plus agents from the FBI, Citizen and Immigration Service, Customs and Border Protection, Secret Service, Coast Guard, and Transportation Safety Agency. The State Department also maintains a Narcotics Affairs Section. The United States has also provided helicopters, drug sniffing dogs, and polygraph units to screen law-enforcement applicants.

U.S. drones spy on cartel hideouts, and U.S. tracking beacons pinpoint suspect's cars and phones. U.S. agents track beacons, trace cell-phone calls, read e-mails, study behavioral patterns of border incursions, follow smuggling routes, and process data about drug dealers, money launderers, and cartel bosses. According to a former Mexican anti-drug prosecutor, U.S. agents are not restricted from eavesdropping on anyone in Mexico by U.S. laws that require judicial authority as long as they are not on U.S. territory and not bugging American citizens.

According to William Wechsler, deputy assistant secretary of defense for counter-narcotics and global threats, the Department of Defense (DOD) will increase its counter-narcotics support for Mexico in fiscal year 2011 (Oct. 1, 2011 to Sept. 30, 2012) to over $50 million. This is a substantial increase from the $34.5 million spent in 2010 and the $34.2 million spent in 2009. Before 2009, the DOD allocated "only" $3 million in U.S. taxpayer funds for Mexican counter-narcotics activities.

Wechsler testified before the Senate Armed Services Emerging Threats and Capabilities Subcommittee on April 12 that the Pentagon's increase in support to Mexico's security forces engaged in the war on drugs will take place despite a recent State Department report of human-rights abuses by Mexican security forces. He also said that the DOD is working "to develop a joint security effort in the border region of Mexico, Guatemala, and Belize."

This DOD assistance is in addition to funds from the State Department that provide training and equipment to Mexican law enforcement to the tune of another $500 million a year appropriated from U.S. taxpayers.

But in spite of all this assistance, President Calderón recently said that U.S. cooperation in the fight against drug cartels has been "insufficient."

I note first of all that whether the government of Mexico chooses to engage in the folly known as the war on drugs is the business of Mexico and Mexicans. Just as no American would appreciate it if some foreign government tried to influence U.S. government policy, so the U.S. government should neither discourage nor encourage the Mexican government to fight a war on drugs or any other activity.

Secondly, if there is nothing in the U.S. Constitution that authorizes the federal government to declare a war on drugs or fight crime, then there is certainly nothing in that document that authorizes the federal government to help Mexico or any other foreign country do those things.

Thirdly, even if Mexico's war on drugs is just and right, the United States should not be funding it. U.S. foreign aid takes many forms, and helping the Mexican government fight drug cartels is just another form of foreign aid. The United States gives billions of dollars in foreign aid every year to many countries. Some receive foreign aid in the billions (like Egypt and Israel) and others receive foreign aid "only" in the millions, tens of millions, or hundreds of millions. But regardless of the amount, foreign-aid spending by the U.S. government is only possible because billions of dollars have first been confiscated from American taxpayers. If an individual American is in favor of the Mexican's government's war on drugs then he can make a contribution to the Mexican government. Just don't expect the rest of us to do likewise.

Fourthly, the government of Mexico should end its war on drugs. Most of the violence and corruption in Mexico is because of the enormous black-market premium in the illicit drug trade. The high risk involved in selling illegal drugs means that drugs sell on the street for many times more than they would sell if drugs were legal. But the war on drugs in Mexico should not be ended just as a way to stop the violence and corruption it fosters. The war on drugs in Mexico should be ended because it is a war on freedom by the Mexican government. Ending the war on drugs in Mexico has nothing to do with surrendering to the drug cartels, appeasing or accommodating them, or just throwing in the towel; it has everything to do with individual liberty, private property, personal responsibility, and the free market.

And finally, the United States should just stop funding and participating in the Mexican drug war. It should likewise end the futile, unconstitutional, expensive, civil-liberties-eroding, financial-privacy-destroying, prison-crowding, and violence-fostering war on drugs.

10

The 40-Year War on Freedom
(*Future of Freedom Foundation Commentaries*, June 15, 2011)

Although the U.S. government's wars in Iraq and Afghanistan have taken center stage for the better part of the last ten years, there is another failed war that has been waged by the federal government for the past forty years.

The war on drugs was declared by President Richard Nixon on June 17, 1971.

Speaking at a press conference in the Briefing Room at the White House, Nixon announced his plan:

> I would like to summarize for you the meeting that I have just had with the bipartisan leaders which began at 8 o'clock and was completed 2 hours later. I began the meeting by making this statement, which I think needs to be made to the Nation: America's public enemy number one in the United States is drug abuse. In order to fight and defeat this enemy, it is necessary to wage a new, all-out offensive.

Nixon left no doubt as to the scope of his offensive:

> This will be a worldwide offensive dealing with the problems of sources of supply, as well as Americans who may be stationed abroad, wherever they are in the world. It will be government wide, pulling together the nine different fragmented areas within the government in which this problem is now being handled, and it will be nationwide in terms of a new educational program that we trust will result from the discussions that we have had.

He went on to say how "essential it was for the American people to be alerted to this danger."

In a special message to the Congress on Drug Abuse Prevention and Control on the same day, Nixon declared drug use to be a "menace," an "increasing grave threat," and a "national emergency."
He also continued his military rhetoric:

> I am transmitting legislation to the Congress to consolidate at the highest level a full-scale attack on the problem of drug abuse in America.
>
> The problems of drug abuse must be faced on many fronts.
>
> To wage an effective war against heroin addiction, we must have international cooperation. In order to secure such cooperation, I am initiating a worldwide escalation in our existing programs for the control of narcotics traffic, and I am proposing a number of new steps for this purpose.
>
> The Comprehensive Drug Abuse Prevention and Control Act of 1970 provides a sound base for the attack on the problem of the availability of narcotics in America.

Nixon then issued Executive Order No. 11599 establishing the Special Action Office of Drug Abuse Prevention (SAODAP) in the Executive Office of the President. He also appointed the first drug czar, Dr. Jerome H. Jaffe, as Special Consultant to the President for Narcotics and Dangerous Drugs.

Nixon's war on drugs really took off after the formation of the Drug Enforcement Agency (DEA) in 1973 and the declaration of an "all-out global war on the drug menace."

This does not mean that the federal government didn't fight against drugs before Nixon declared his war. To the contrary, the feds have waged war on personal freedom via the drug war since the passage in 1905 of the first federal anti-narcotics law aimed at ending the opium trade in the Philippines.

This was followed by the Pure Food and Drug Act of 1906, the Opium Exclusion Act of 1909, the Harrison Narcotics Tax Act of 1914, the Marijuana Tax Act of 1937, the Narcotic Control Act of 1956, and the Comprehensive Drug Abuse

Prevention and Control Act of 1970.

And since the beginning of Nixon's war, we have had the Anti-Drug Abuse Act of 1986, the Anti-Drug Abuse Act of 1988, the Chemical Diversion and Trafficking Act of 1988, the Illicit Drug Anti-Proliferation Act of 2003, and the Combat Methamphetamine Epidemic Act of 2005.

And who can forget the D.A.R.E. school-lecture program, "Just Say No" clubs, and the Partnership for a Drug-Free America's television ad featuring a hot skillet, an egg, and the phrase, "This is your brain on drugs."

The case against the drug war has been made so many times that, at the risk of sounding like a broken record, I will limit myself to ten key points:

- The war on drugs costs American taxpayers over $40 billion a year.
- For the first half of our nation's history there were no prohibitions against any drug.
- The war on drugs is not authorized by the Constitution.
- Tobacco kills more people every year than all of the people killed by all illegal drugs in the twentieth century.
- The war on drugs has done nothing to reduce the demand for illicit drugs.
- Numerous studies have shown that smoking marijuana is less dangerous than drinking alcohol.
- The war on drugs is the cause of our unnecessarily swelled prison populations.
- Alcohol abuse, not drug abuse, is one of the leading causes of premature deaths in the United States.
- The war on drugs has ruined more lives than drugs themselves.
- More people in America die every year from drugs prescribed and administered by physicians than from illegal drugs.

To drug warriors, these things don't matter: Because taking drugs is bad for one's health and morally corrupting, the state has the duty to regulate and ban them.

But as true and important as these things are, the drug-warrior statists are right about dismissing them for in the end they really don't matter. And there are many other things that don't matter as well.

It doesn't matter if the drug war can or can't be "won." It doesn't matter if drug addiction destroys or doesn't destroy lives and families. It doesn't matter if marijuana is or isn't a gateway drug. It doesn't matter if the majority of Americans support or don't support the drug war. It doesn't matter if marijuana is or isn't beneficial for pain management. It doesn't matter if fighting the drug war is or isn't a bipartisan issue. It doesn't matter if cocaine and heroin are or aren't addictive. It doesn't matter if drug use would or wouldn't increase if drugs were legalized. It doesn't matter if advocates for drug decriminalization want or don't want to get high. It doesn't matter if smoking crack is or isn't dangerous. It doesn't matter if drug use is or isn't immoral. It doesn't matter if the war on drugs is or isn't "worth it."

What matters is personal freedom, private property, personal responsibility, individual liberty, personal and financial privacy, free markets, limited government, and the natural right to be left alone if one is not aggressing against his someone and is doing "anything that's peaceful."

Ending the war on drugs is not an esoteric issue of libertarians or a pet issue of those who want to get high. Once the government claims control over what a man smokes, snorts, sniffs, inhales, or otherwise ingests into his body, there is no limit to its power. As the economist Ludwig von Mises so eloquently said: "As soon as we surrender the principle that the state should not interfere in any questions touching on the individual's mode of life, we end by regulating and restricting the latter down to the smallest detail." The war on drugs is incompatible with a free society.

11

The War on Drugs Is Senseless
(Future of Freedom Foundation Commentaries, August 23, 2011)*

The war on drugs is a failure. It has failed to prevent drug abuse. It has failed to keep drugs out of the hands of addicts. It has failed to keep drugs away from teenagers. It has failed to reduce the demand for drugs. It has failed to stop the violence associated with drug trafficking. It has failed to help drug addicts get treatment.

But the war on drugs has also succeeded. It has succeeded in clogging the judicial system. It has succeeded in swelling prison populations. It has succeeded in corrupting law enforcement. It has succeeded in destroying financial privacy. It has succeeded in militarizing the police. It has succeeded in hindering legitimate pain treatment. It has succeeded in destroying the Fourth Amendment. It has succeeded in eroding civil liberties. It has succeeded in making criminals out of hundreds of thousands of law-abiding Americans. It has succeeded in wasting hundreds of billions of taxpayer dollars. It has succeeded in ruining countless lives.

Clearly, the financial and human costs of the drug war far exceed any of its supposed benefits. Clearly, the drug war violates the Constitution and exceeds the proper role of government. And clearly, the drug war is a war on personal freedom, private property, personal responsibility, individual liberty, personal and financial privacy, and the free market.

But the war on drugs is also something else. It is the most senseless of the government's wars.

The Food and Drug Administration recently released nine new warning labels that will soon be appearing on packs of cigarettes. The new graphic labels will replace the four familiar and smaller text warnings that have appeared on cigarette

49

packages for the past 25 years.

The United States was the first country to require health warnings on packs of cigarettes.

The original warning label, appearing on cigarette packs from 1966 to 1970, was "Caution: Cigarette Smoking May be Hazardous to Your Health." It was replaced from 1970 to 1985 with "Warning: The Surgeon General Has Determined that Cigarette Smoking is Dangerous to Your Health."

Since 1985, cigarette packs have contained one of four surgeon-general's warnings:

- SURGEON GENERAL'S WARNING: Smoking Causes Lung Cancer, Heart Disease, Emphysema, And May Complicate Pregnancy.
- SURGEON GENERAL'S WARNING: Quitting Smoking Now Greatly Reduces Serious Risks to Your Health.
- SURGEON GENERAL'S WARNING: Smoking By Pregnant Women May Result in Fetal Injury, Premature Birth, And Low Birth Weight.
- SURGEON GENERAL'S WARNING: Cigarette Smoke Contains Carbon Monoxide.

The new labels, which cigarette makers must begin using by the fall of 2012, will take up the top half on both sides of a pack of cigarettes.

The images appearing with the warnings will show rotting teeth and gums, a man with a tracheotomy smoking, diseased lungs, the corpse of a smoker, a mother holding her baby with smoke swirling around them, a premature baby, a woman crying, someone breathing with an oxygen mask, and an ex-smoker wearing an "I Quit" T-shirt.

The gruesome graphics are accompanied by one of the following text warnings:

- Smoking can kill you.
- Cigarettes cause cancer.
- Cigarettes cause strokes and heart disease.

- Cigarettes cause fatal lung disease.
- Cigarettes are addictive.
- Tobacco smoke can harm your children.
- Tobacco smoke causes fatal lung disease in nonsmokers.
- Quitting smoking now greatly reduces serious risks to your health.
- Smoking during pregnancy can harm your baby.

Each label also includes a national "quit-smoking" hotline number (1-800-QUIT-NOW).

The new labels are the result of the Family Smoking Prevention and Tobacco Control Act (PL 111-31). This legislation passed the Senate on June 11, 2009, by a vote of 79-17. It passed the House on June 12, 2009, by a vote of 307- 97. There were 22 Republicans in the Senate and 70 in the House that supported this nanny-state legislation that gave the FDA the legal authority to regulate tobacco. Thanks, "free-market, less-government" Republicans.

The new labels "are frank, honest and powerful depictions of the health risks of smoking," said Health and Human Services Secretary Kathleen Sebelius.

The FDA says the introduction of the new warnings "is expected to have a significant public health impact by decreasing the number of smokers, resulting in lives saved, increased life expectancy, and lower medical costs."

Health advocacy groups praised the new labels as well. American Cancer Society CEO John R. Seffrin issued a statement saying that the labels have the potential to "encourage adults to give up their deadly addiction to cigarettes and deter children from starting in the first place."

Figures vary, but tobacco use is supposed to cost the U.S. economy nearly $200 billion annually in medical costs and lost productivity and causes more than 440,000 premature deaths each year from heart disease, stroke, cancer, or smoking-related diseases.

So what does all that have to do with the war on drugs? It looks like the government has a war on tobacco as well. True, but there are some important differences.

One, smoking cigarettes is still legal. Anyone can buy as many cigarettes as he wants and smoke as many as he wants without fear that government at any level will hinder him from doing so. He may not have the freedom to smoke in a bar or restaurant, but that is another topic for another article.

Two, in spite of its warning labels and anti-smoking campaigns, the federal government doesn't really want all smokers to quit lighting up. The government needs the revenue it gets from taxing tobacco. There is currently a federal excise tax of $1.01 per pack on regular "class A" cigarettes. Larger "Class B" cigarettes are taxed twice as much. And then there are the taxes on cigars, chewing tobacco, snuff, pipe tobacco, loose cigarette tobacco, and rolling papers. (States and some localities also tax tobacco products).

Three, and what really shows the senselessness of the war on drugs, smoking tobacco is actually very bad for your health. Although I oppose the government's war on tobacco as much as I oppose the government's war on drugs, that doesn't change the fact that using tobacco is harmful and a major contributor to the major causes of death in the United States (heart disease, cancer, stroke, and chronic respiratory diseases).

If the federal government is going to make a harmful substance illegal, then it seems logical that that substance should be tobacco. It is the cultivation, processing, sale, and use of tobacco that should be illicit, not marijuana. The number of deaths attributable every year to marijuana smoking is a big fat zero. And marijuana does have some known health benefits. If smoking cigarettes causes cancer; causes strokes and heart disease; causes fatal lung disease; is addictive; harms fetuses, children, and nonsmokers; poses serious risks to your health; and kills you, then it only makes sense to criminalize tobacco instead of marijuana.

But what about other illicit drugs such as LSD, cocaine, heroin, and methamphetamine? There is no question that deaths have occurred from the use of those drugs. But more than 100,000 people die every year from drugs prescribed and administered by physicians. And more than two million Americans a year have in-hospital adverse drug reactions. Thousands of people die every year from reactions to aspirin.

In my state of Florida, the *Orlando Sentinel* just reported on July 6, 2011, that, according to a report by the Centers for Disease Control and Prevention, the prescription-drug death rate increased by 84.2 percent from 2003-2009. The Oxycodone death rate was up 265 percent. The Xanax death rate was up 234 percent. Yet, the illegal-drugs death rate was down 21 percent to 3.4 deaths per 100,000 Floridians.

The number of annual deaths caused by all drugs—legal and illegal—pales in comparison with deaths caused by tobacco. And likewise the costs to society and the economy. If smoking tobacco is as bad as the government says it is, then it only makes sense to ban the cultivation, processing, sale, and use of tobacco, and to do so immediately. It is tobacco traffickers who should be sentenced to long prison terms. It is tobacco dealers who should be arrested and whose lives should be ruined. It is tobacco peddlers who should be fined and scorned. It is tobacco users whose property should be confiscated.

Now, lest there be any misunderstanding, I am not in favor of any government at any level banning tobacco. That is because I am not in favor of any government at any level banning the buying, selling, growing, processing, use, or possession of any substance. And that is because, as a libertarian, I believe in individual liberty and personal responsibility instead of a nanny state run by bureaucrats looking out for my health and safety.

The war on drugs is senseless, just as a war on any other substance would be.

12

The Other Unconstitutional War
(*The New American*, November 7, 2011)

It wasn't long after World War II ended that U.S. troops were once again involved in another foreign war. This time, however, there was a notable difference. After North Korea invaded the South in 1950, President Truman intervened with U.S. combat troops in a United Nations "police action." There was no congressional declaration of war. There was not even the slightest pretense of consulting Congress.

On five different occasions, the United States had declared war on other countries: the War of 1812, the Mexican War (1848), the Spanish-American War (1898), World War I (1917), and World War II (1941 against Japan, Germany, and Italy; 1942 against Bulgaria, Hungary, and Romania).

That Congress issued these declarations of war doesn't necessarily mean that they should have been issued. It just means that it was recognized that a major military engagement called for a real declaration of war by the Congress according to Article I, Section 8, of the Constitution.

But not only did over 36,000 American soldiers needlessly die in the Korean War when we entered that conflict under the auspices of the UN, the results of this unconstitutional action are still with us today. Since the armistice was signed in 1953, a day has not gone by when the United States has not had thousands of troops stationed in South Korea. There are at least 25,000 U.S. soldiers still in Korea, some no doubt the grandchildren of the soldiers who fought in the Korean War.

But this Korean intervention also set a terrible precedent, as no declaration of war has ever been issued since World War II even though the United States has been involved in many military conflicts since then, with some of them being major wars like Vietnam, Iraq, and Afghanistan.

A War for Our Own Good

Aside from U.S. military operations in Iraq, Afghanistan, Pakistan, Yemen, Somalia, Libya, and now Uganda, there is currently raging another destructive and unconstitutional war at home. And this one has been going on for over forty years.

It was just over 40 years ago that President Richard Nixon began the federal war on drugs. Said Nixon: "In order to fight and defeat this enemy, it is necessary to wage a new, all-out offensive." The President declared drug abuse to be "America's public enemy number one" and "a national emergency." He continued his military rhetoric in a special message to Congress on drug abuse prevention and control, calling for a "full-scale attack" on drug abuse "on many fronts." To wage "an effective war against heroin addiction," he called for "a worldwide escalation in our existing programs for the control of narcotics traffic." Legislation then recently passed in Congress provided "a sound base for the attack on the problem of the availability of narcotics in America."

None of this means that the federal government didn't fight against drugs and drug abuse before Nixon. Although all drugs in the United States were legal up until the 20th century, the federal government began introducing anti-narcotics laws in 1905. It was Nixon, though, that formally declared war on drugs, appointed the first drug czar, and oversaw the establishment of the Drug Enforcement Agency (DEA) in 1973. The drug war escalated again under President Ronald Reagan in the 1980s with his wife's "Just Say No" campaign. Although 15 states and the District of Columbia have legalized marijuana for medical use, the federal war on drugs continues unabated and enjoys wide bipartisan support.

But what has the decades-long federal war on drugs actually accomplished? How much has it cost? Has it curtailed drug abuse? Has it, in fact, been any more successful at curtailing drug abuse than Prohibition was at curtailing alcohol abuse? Why, unlike Prohibition, was it imposed without a constitutional amendment granting the government the power to do what it is doing? And should the power even be granted through the amendment process, or should the federal war on drugs be ended?

Another Failure

Even though the federal war against alcohol known as Prohibition was constitutional owing to the 18th Amendment, most Americans would today undoubtedly agree that its repeal via the 21st Amendment was a good thing. But all of the unconstitutional wars the federal government is now waging—including its war on drugs—should be ended as well.

Like Prohibition, the war on drugs is a failure. It has failed to prevent drug abuse or reduce the demand for drugs. It has failed to keep drugs out of the hands of addicts and away from teenagers. It has failed to stop the flow of drugs into the United States. According to the latest National Survey on Drug Use and Health conducted by the Substance Abuse and Mental Health Services Administration: "Drug use in the United States increased in 2009, reversing downward trends since 2002." There was even a spike in the number of Americans admitting to using ecstasy and methamphetamine. The government's own Government Accountability Office has even said that the anti-drug D.A.R.E. program has had "no statistically significant long-term effect on preventing youth illicit drug use."

But that's not all.

The costs of the war on drugs exceed its benefits. According to a study released last year by the Cato Institute, spending on the drug war tops $41 billion a year.

The war on drugs has clogged the federal court system. Chief Justice William Rehnquist made this point as far back as 1989. And in testimony before the Senate Judiciary Committee last month, Supreme Court Justice Antonin Scalia remarked that "it was a great mistake to put routine drug offenses into the federal courts."

The war on drugs makes criminals out of too many otherwise law-abiding Americans. The DEA made almost 31,000 arrests last year. According to the FBI's latest report on "Crime in the United States," over 1.6 million Americans were arrested on drug charges in 2010, with almost half of those arrests just for marijuana possession. There is one drug arrest in the United States every 19 seconds.

The war on drugs unnecessarily swells prison populations. Over half of the federal prison population and about 20 percent of the state prison population are imprisoned due to the drug war.

The war on drugs hinders legitimate pain management. Physicians that specialize in pain treatment face the increasing danger of arrest by the DEA for prescribing their patients a dose of painkillers higher than some government-set maximum.

The war on drugs has resulted in gross absurdities. Due to the Combat Methamphetamine Epidemic Act, which is title VII of the USA PATRIOT Improvement and Reauthorization Act of 2005, over-the-counter allergy-relief products like Sudafed have been rationed and their use criminalized because they contain pseudoephedrine, which might be used in the illegal manufacture of methamphetamine.

The war on drugs has destroyed financial privacy. Deposit more than $10,000 in a bank account and you are a suspected drug trafficker. Travelers carrying what the government thinks is too large an amount of cash are subject to harassment and having their property confiscated.

The war on drugs has provided the rationale for militarizing local police forces. The Pentagon has transferred millions of pieces of surplus military gear to local police departments. The majority of the 130-150 raids per day conducted by SWAT teams are to serve search warrants on people suspected of drug crimes.

The war on drugs has resulted in outrageous behavior by police in their quest to arrest drug dealers. The city of Daytona Beach Shores was recently ordered to pay four dancers and two bartenders (and their attorneys) a total of $195,000 to settle a federal lawsuit after they were illegally strip-searched during a raid on their club. The women were strip-searched in front of a group of male officers after police were told that some employees were selling prescription pills and other illegal narcotics to patrons. A federal judge found that "the search warrant did not authorize a strip search of anyone in the club."

Picking Up New Powers

The war on drugs has eviscerated the Fourth Amendment's prohibition against unreasonable searches and seizures. In the recent Supreme Court case of *Kentucky v. King*, police were exonerated for kicking in the door of the wrong apartment while they were making a "controlled buy" of crack cocaine after they supposedly "smelled marijuana," "could hear people inside moving," and believed that "drug related evidence was about to be destroyed."

The war on drugs has increased the size and scope of government. The DEA has 10,000 employees in 226 offices organized in 21 divisions throughout the United States and 83 foreign offices in 63 countries around the world. There are even 300 chemists employed by the DEA. The DEA's Office of Aviation Operations has 100 airplanes and 124 pilots.

The war on drugs has served as a pretext for a war on individual liberty and private property. According to Austrian economist Ludwig von Mises:

> Opium and morphine are certainly dangerous, habit-forming drugs. But once the principle is admitted that it is the duty of government to protect the individual against his own foolishness, no serious objections can be advanced against further encroachments.

> As soon as we surrender the principle that the state should not interfere in any questions touching on the individual's mode of life, we end by regulating and restricting the latter down to the smallest detail.

Mises did not believe that government at any level should interject itself into "the individual's mode of life." America's Founding Fathers did allow for some government involvement concerning the lives of the people in the federal system they created—but not at the national level. In *The Federalist*, No. 45, Madison summarized the division of powers between states and the federal government this way:

> The powers delegated by the proposed Constitution to the federal government, are few and defined. Those which are to remain in the State governments are numerous and indefinite. The former will be exercised principally on external objects, as war, peace, negotiation, and foreign commerce; with which last the power of taxation will, for the most part, be connected. The powers reserved to the several States will extend to all the objects which, in the ordinary course of affairs, concern the lives, liberties, and properties of the people, and the internal order, improvement, and prosperity of the State.

Under the federal system devised by the Founding Fathers, the national government is quite libertarian, while state governments are less so. But the existence of multiple state governments, each operating under their own state constitution, provides an important check against enactment of "numerous and indefinite laws"—including drug laws—to the point where the "individual's mode of life" is restricted "down to the smallest detail." This is true not only because the actions of a single state could not destroy the liberties of the entire nation, but also because of the ability of individuals and businesses to move from one state to another if a state were to become too repressive, thereby encouraging states not to go too far in their taxation or regulation policies.

Of course, this system is not working as intended because the federal government has unconstitutionally usurped powers never intended for the federal level, and the states are acting as if they are mere regional subdivisions of the national government. The usurped powers include those being used to wage the war on drugs, which entails Soviet-style central planning by the federal government. Just as the government has a calculation problem when it comes to central planning of the economy, so also with drug regulation. The government can only arbitrarily decide which drugs should be legal and which drugs shouldn't be, which drugs should be available to minors and which drugs shouldn't be, which drugs should be regulated and which drugs shouldn't be, which drugs should be sold by prescription and which drugs should be available over the counter, which drugs should be classified as Schedule I and which drugs should be classified as Schedule II, etc. The drug war fosters too much trust in government planners, regulators, and bureaucrats.

None of these things matter to drug warriors, however, because taking drugs is unhealthy and immoral. While I don't deny the truth of those conclusions in regard to non-medicinal drug usage, advocating a federal war on drugs for these reasons teems with hypocrisy.

Facts Flying in the Face of Drug Laws

Figures vary, but tobacco use is supposed to cost the U.S. economy nearly $200 billion annually in medical costs and lost productivity and causes over 440,000 premature deaths each year from heart disease, stroke, cancer, and chronic respiratory diseases. The number of annual deaths caused by all drugs—legal and illegal—pales in comparison to deaths caused by tobacco. It seems rather senseless for the federal government to wage war on drugs instead of on tobacco.

Every negative thing that could be said regarding drug abuse could also be said of alcohol abuse—and even more so. Alcohol abuse is one of the leading causes of premature death in the United States. Alcohol is a factor in many drownings, child abuse cases, sex crimes, violent crimes, divorces, suicides, fires, and home, boating, and car accidents. According to a study recently published in the prestigious medical journal *The Lancet*, alcohol ranks as the "most harmful drug," beating out heroin, crack cocaine, and ecstasy. Yet, it is only the decriminalization of drugs that conservatives like Bill Bennett call "stupid and morally atrocious."

And then there are the dangers of prescription drugs—that is, drugs the government says are safe and legal. According to various articles in the *Journal of the American Medical Association*, over 100,000 people die every year from drugs prescribed and administered by physicians. And over two million Americans a year have in-hospital adverse drug reactions. Thousands of people die every year from harmful reactions to aspirin.

One doesn't have to be a libertarian to recognize that the federal war on drugs is a monstrous evil—incompatible with private property, individual liberty, personal responsibility, free markets, and limited government—and an illogical and hypocritical activity of the federal government.

One of the most powerful arguments against the federal war on drugs, and one that has the broadest possible appeal, is the fact that a federal drug war is blatantly unconstitutional. The powers delegated to the national government are, as Madison said, "few and defined." Everything else is reserved to the states. And just to reinforce this federal arrangement, the 10th Amendment declares that "the powers not delegated to the United States by the Constitution, nor prohibited by it to the States, are reserved to the States respectively, or to the people."

The Constitution nowhere authorizes the national government to prohibit, regulate, or otherwise concern itself with the nature, quantity, or production of any substance Americans wish to inhale, inject, or otherwise ingest into their bodies.

When the federal government sought to limit the use of alcoholic beverages after World War I, it realized that it could only do so by amending the Constitution. That is why the 18th Amendment to the Constitution was adopted in 1919. If a constitutional amendment was needed to prohibit the "manufacture, sale, or transportation of intoxicating liquors," then it should also be necessary in order for the federal government to prohibit other substances like hallucinogenic drugs.

Strong Stances

One of the few members of Congress who actually tries to follow the Constitution in this matter is Representative and Republican presidential candidate Ron Paul. Rep. Paul has cosponsored a bill, the Ending Federal Marijuana Prohibition Act of 2011 (H.R. 2306), to end the federal ban on marijuana, not because he is a supporter of drug use, wants more kids to try marijuana, or is indifferent to the dangers of illicit drugs, but because he is a strict constitutionalist, a believer in individual liberty and personal responsibility, and an advocate of restoring the limited government established by the Founders.

Most members of Congress just don't get it because they see themselves as nannies and overseers entrusted to use the power of the federal government to stamp out vice and keep Americans healthy and safe because they are too stupid to take care of themselves.

Typical is Lamar Smith (R-Texas), House Judiciary Committee Chairman, who vowed to block Paul's bill. "Instead of encouraging the use of marijuana," said Smith, "we should strengthen enforcement of federal drug laws to protect Americans from the devastating effects of drug use." There is, unfortunately, wide bipartisan support in Congress for continuing the federal war on drugs for another 40 years.

It is members of Congress like Smith that are more dangerous to Americans than illegal drugs. As C. S. Lewis has written:

> Of all tyrannies a tyranny sincerely exercised for the good of its victims may be the most oppressive. It may be better to live under robber barons than under omnipotent moral busybodies. The robber baron's cruelty may sometimes sleep, his cupidity may at some point be satiated; but those who torment us for our own good will torment us without end for they do so with the approval of their own conscience.

If any war on drugs is to be fought, it will have to be on the state level. Any laws or regulations relating to the production, sale, distribution, possession, or use of drugs—whether we agree with them or not—should be passed by state legislatures, not the U.S. Congress or its agents like the FDA, DEA, or the Office of National Drug Control Policy. No American who has any respect for the Constitution, federalism, and the limited government established by the Founders should endorse, support, or defend the federal war on drugs, regardless of his political persuasion, religion, or moral code.

13

Drug Testing for Welfare Benefits
(*Future of Freedom Foundation Commentaries*, November 15, 2011)

Lawmakers in dozens of states are considering proposals to require drug testing of welfare recipients. In these days of budget tightening, states are looking for ways to balance their budgets without raising taxes. The drug-testing requirements are supposed to save the states money, since they will cause some families to be prohibited from receiving welfare benefits.

The proposed measures seem to resonate with the public and are especially popular with Republican legislators. The constitutionality of such laws, however, is in question.

A 1999 law in Michigan that instituted random drug testing for those receiving state benefits was halted by a federal judge after it had been in effect only five weeks. A federal appeals court eventually found the law unconstitutional in 2003, finding that it violated the Fourth Amendment's protection against unreasonable search and seizure.

One state that is again testing the waters with mandatory drug testing to receive welfare benefits is my state of Florida. Introduced in January 2011, HB 353 passed the Florida House by a vote of 78-38 on April 26 and the Senate by a vote of 26-11 on May 4. The bill was signed into law by Florida's governor, Rick Scott, on May 31, with an effective date of July 1.

"Drug Screening of Potential and Existing Beneficiaries of Temporary Assistance for Needy Families" (TANF) requires the Florida Department of Children and Family Services to

> perform drug test on applicant for TANF benefits; requires such individual to bear cost of drug test; requires department to provide, & applicant to acknowledge receipt of, notice of drug-screening policy; requires department to increase amount of initial TANF benefit by amount paid by

individual for drug testing; provides procedures for testing & retesting; requires department to provide information concerning local substance abuse treatment programs to individual who tests positive; provides conditions for reapplication for TANF benefits; provides that, if parent is ineligible as result of failing drug test, eligibility of children is not affected; provides for designation of another protective payee; provides rulemaking authority to department.

TANF is the 1996 successor to Aid to Families with Dependent Children (AFDC). It is a federal program that is administered by the states by means of federal block grants ($16.5 billion in FY2011). Seventeen states also qualify for more than $300 million in supplemental grants. Counting both grants, the state of Florida receives more than $600 million a year from the federal government for the TANF program.

Floridians who qualify for the program can receive a cash payment of $180 a month for one person or $364 for a family of four.

Applicants who fail the drug test are banned from receiving benefits for one year. A second failure results in a three-year ban. However, anyone who tests positive and is denied TANF benefits as a result may reapply after six months if he can document the successful completion of a substance-abuse treatment program. There is a provision in the law that lets parents name a guardian to receive benefits (after passing a drug test) in behalf of the children.

It is "unfair for Florida taxpayers to subsidize drug addiction," said Governor Scott. "It's the right thing for citizens of this state that need public assistance. We don't want to waste tax dollars," he added.

The ACLU disagreed, however, and filed suit to block the Florida law on behalf of a Navy veteran who was denied financial assistance from the state to help care for his four-year-old son because he refused to take a drug test. Like the previous case in Michigan, the ACLU is arguing that the law is unconstitutional because it constitutes an unreasonable search or seizure.

A federal judge has just temporarily blocked the new Florida law, saying that it may violate the Constitution's ban on unreasonable searches and seizures. The injunction will stay in place until the judge holds a full hearing on the matter.

Speaking on NPR's *Talk of the Nation* recently about the issue of drug testing as a prerequisite for welfare benefits, Barry McCaffrey, the former head of the White House Office of National Drug Control Policy (Bill Clinton's drug czar), expressed his opposition to the policy: "I don't think that having a drug-testing program that's a bar to entry to welfare or food stamps makes sense where you don't tie it to effective drug treatment. And even then, I'd want to see some probability that you exhibited drug behavior before I test you."

So, should states require that applicants for, or recipients of, welfare benefits take a drug test?

From a libertarian standpoint, the answer is neither—no drug tests and no welfare benefits.

But first, as a practical matter, the proposal—at least in Florida—is absurd. One, there is no requirement that a recipient of cash assistance be tested again after his initial test. Someone could pass the test, be judged drug-free, and then use the money he receives for drugs throughout the 48 months he is allowed to receive TANF cash assistance. Two, there is nothing preventing a Florida recipient of cash assistance from using his money to buy alcohol, purchase pornography, procure a prostitute, or gamble it away at one of the Florida Indian casinos. Three, at $30 to $35 per test, the drug-testing program could cost the state of Florida many thousands of dollars. Since the law's implementation, the Florida Department of Children and Families has tested 1,500 to 2,000 recipients. About 2.5 percent of applicants tested positive and about 2 percent declined to be tested. That means that the state of Florida has had to reimburse about 95.5 percent of applicants for their drug test. And four, there is the constitutional question whether the drug-testing requirement constitutes an unreasonable search.

In a libertarian society, that is, a free society based on voluntary cooperation and contracts instead of government coercion and regulations, all drugs would be legal. However, employers, business establishments, and property owners would have the right to prohibit all drugs or certain drugs from being on or in the body of employees, customers, and visitors. That might include scheduled or random drug testing as a condition of employment, doing business, or visiting because in a free society any lawful property occupier—employer, business establishment, or private individual—has the right to allow or prohibit anyone access to his property for any reason.

But without the government's war on freedom known as the war on drugs, I suspect that most of the drug testing that takes place now would be a thing of the past. Perhaps airlines would test pilots and taxi companies would test drivers—but they would not be required to do so by a government.

The larger issue here—and one that is just as important from a constitutional perspective—is the legitimacy of welfare benefits in the first place. Conservatives who support drug testing as a prerequisite to receiving welfare benefits are only scratching the surface if they are trying to reduce the welfare rolls. In fact, crusading for drug tests allows conservatives to appear fiscally conservative and in favor of reducing the welfare state without actually alienating great numbers of potential voters who are either on welfare or sympathetic toward those who are.

Governor Scott said it was "unfair for Florida taxpayers to subsidize drug addiction." What he didn't say—and what Democrats and most Republicans won't say—is that it is unfair for Florida taxpayers (or U.S. taxpayers) to subsidize anyone or anything. No personal welfare and no corporate welfare.

In his remarks on January 15, 1964, to the leaders of organizations concerned with the problems of senior citizens, President Lyndon Johnson said, "We are going to try to take all the money that we think is unnecessarily being spent and take it from the 'haves' and give it to the 'have nots' that need it so much."

Conservatives in Florida or anywhere else who remain silent about welfare programs subsidizing one group of people at the expense of another are silently endorsing the legitimacy of Johnson's attempts to redistribute wealth under the guise of a war on poverty.

As the successor to the AFDC program, the modern TANF is a New Deal/Great Society-type program that takes money from those who have and gives it to those who have not. It is a wealth-punishing, social-engineering, income-transfer program. Which means it is no different from other income-redistribution schemes such as Supplemental Security Income (SSI), energy assistance, Medicare, Medicaid, State Children's Health Insurance Program (SCHIP), unemployment compensation, food stamps (now called the Supplemental Nutrition Assistance Program, or SNAP), and the refundable Earned Income Tax Credit (EITC).

Rather than on excluding a few people from receiving the wealth of others because they failed a drug test, efforts should be focused on eliminating the income-transfer programs that make welfare possible.

14

Drug-Sentencing Disparities

(Future of Freedom Foundation Commentaries, November 22, 2011)

As many as 12,000 inmates in federal prison could soon be released early—including 1,800 who are eligible for immediate release—thanks to the U.S. Sentencing Commission's vote earlier this year to provide retroactive application of the Fair Sentencing Act that was passed by Congress last year. The new policy took effect on November 1.

Does that mean that murderers and armed robbers will now be roaming the streets to prey on us? Not at all. The prisoners eligible for early release are those incarcerated for the "crime" of possessing drugs.

The Anti-Drug Abuse Act of 1986 established, among other punishments for drug "crimes," a disparity of 100:1 between federal penalties for crack cocaine and powder cocaine. The Act also instituted a five-year mandatory minimum sentence for first-time possession of five grams of crack cocaine.

Critics of the Act have viewed the disparity as racially discriminatory because black drug offenders are more likely to be charged with crack possession and therefore serve longer prison terms than white offenders.

After numerous legal challenges, proposed legislation, and recommendations over the years to reduce this sentencing disparity, the Fair Sentencing Act (S.1789) was passed by the U.S. Senate on March 17, 2010, by unanimous consent, and by the House of Representatives on July 27, 2010, by voice vote. The bill became Public Law 111-220 after being signed by Barack Obama on August 3, 2010.

The Fair Sentencing Act amended the Controlled Substances Act by increasing the amount of crack cocaine required for the imposition of mandatory minimum prison terms for trafficking (from 5 to 28 grams) and directed the U.S. Sentencing Commission to, among other things, "promulgate guidelines, policy statements, or amendments required by this Act as soon as practicable, but not later than 90 days after the enactment of this Act."

On October 15, 2010, the U.S. Sentencing Commission voted to amend federal sentencing guidelines to reflect the changes made by the Fair Sentencing Act. On June 30, 2011, the Commission voted to make the changes retroactive beginning on November 1, 2011.

The sentencing disparity for possessing crack versus powder cocaine is now 18:1 instead of 100:1. The average federal sentence for crack cocaine offenses will still be about 127 months, according to Judge Patti B. Saris of the Federal District Court in Boston.

But that is not good enough, according to opponents of the Fair Sentencing Act.

Predictably, the Fraternal Order of Police and the National Sheriffs' Association opposed the Act. The NSA even supported increasing the prison sentence for powder cocaine "rather than significantly reducing the sentence for crack cocaine."

Lamar Smith (R-Tex.), House Judiciary Committee chairman, actually argued that the Act would hurt minorities instead of eliminate the institutionalized racism that the sentencing disparities have engendered:

> Why would we want to reduce the penalties for crack cocaine trafficking and invite a return to a time when cocaine ravaged our communities, especially minority communities? This bill sends the wrong message to drug dealers and those who traffic in destroying Americans' lives. It sends the message that Congress takes drug crimes less seriously than they did. The bill before us threatens to return America to the days when crack cocaine corroded the minds and bodies of our children, decimated a generation, and destroyed communities.

Smith has also expressed his opposition to a bill (H.R.2306) coauthored by Ron Paul, the Ending Federal Marijuana Prohibition Act of 2011, that would end the federal ban on marijuana.

Drug warriors aren't happy about the retroactive application of the Fair Sentencing Act, either.

William Otis, a former federal prosecutor and special White House counsel under George H.W. Bush, maintained that the early releases would inevitably lead to more crime.

Lamar Smith issued a statement expressing his disapproval:

> Nothing in the Act nor in the congressional record implies that Congress ever intended that the new crack cocaine guidelines should be applied retroactively. And yet, the Sentencing Commission may release thousands of crack traffickers before they have fully served their sentences.

The war on drugs has made criminals out of many otherwise law-abiding Americans and unnecessarily swelled prison populations.

The DEA made almost 31,000 arrests last year. According to the FBI's latest "Crime in the United States," report, more than 1.6 million Americans were arrested on drug charges in 2010, with almost half of those arrests just for marijuana possession. There is one drug arrest in the United States every 19 seconds.

The United States leads the world in the incarceration rate and in the total prison population. According to the Department of Justice's Bureau of Justice Statistics Bulletin "Prisoners in 2009" (the latest year available), there were, on December 31, 2009, 1,613,740 prisoners under the jurisdiction of state or federal correctional authorities, with 1,405,622 in state prisons and 208,118 in federal prisons. Almost 20 percent of the state prison population are incarcerated because of drug charges. Almost half of the federal prison population are incarcerated because of drug charges. There are almost 350,000 Americans in state or federal prison at this moment because of drug charges.

Some members of law enforcement oppose the liberty-destroying war on drugs. Law Enforcement against

Prohibition, or LEAP, is an international organization of criminal-justice professionals who favor a repeal of drug-prohibition laws. In Sacramento, California, A group of police officers, prosecutors, judges, and other criminal-justice professionals have endorsed the Regulate Marijuana Like Wine Act of 2012, a ballot initiative to end marijuana prohibition in California and regulate the sale of marijuana the same way the wine industry is regulated.

By means of the Controlled Substances Act of 1970, the federal government has classified hundreds of drugs as controlled substances and ranked them on five schedules on the basis of their potential for abuse and currently accepted medical uses. The well-known drugs diacetylmorphine (heroin); d-lysergic acid diethylamide (LSD); marijuana; 3,4-methylene-dioxymethamphetamine (ecstasy); and methamphetamine (meth) are classified as Schedule I controlled substances, while drugs such as amphetamine (speed), morphine, oxycodone (Oxy-Contin), and cocaine are classified as Schedule II controlled substances.

Although most illicit drugs are used for the same basic purpose (to get high or alter the mood in some way), there are a myriad of penalties for mere possession, or possession without a prescription, of the various controlled substances and trafficking or dealing (terms the government uses instead of "selling" to make them sound ominous) in controlled substances. Sentences can vary widely depending on the drug type and amount, along with other mitigating circumstances. That is, sentencing for drug crimes is extremely arbitrary in nature—like the sentencing disparity for crack and powder cocaine that was just reduced.

Trafficking in Schedule I drugs, even for first-time, nonviolent offenders, can result in a defendant's being put away in prison longer than hijacking, kidnapping, or rape when multiple sales are "stacked" in one proceeding, and especially when a gun is found on the defendant, whether he brandished it or not.

In the case of *United States v. Angelos* (2006), Weldon Angelos was accused of selling marijuana to a police informant on several occasions over a period of a few weeks. Because of the mandatory minimum sentences for possessing a firearm during a drug deal, Angelos—who had no prior convictions—was sentenced to 55 years of mandatory prison time in addition to the drug charges, which were later reduced to one day. And because there is no parole in the federal prison system, he effectively received a life sentence for selling marijuana. He lost on appeal, the Supreme Court declined to hear the case, and a federal judge denied his request for a new trial.

Federal judge Roger Vinson, expressing his concern over an earlier similar case in which a defendant receiving an additional 45 years in prison because he possessed a gun during a series of controlled buys, reasoned that "because the case involved controlled buys, the government had complete and unfettered discretion to increase the defendant's mandatory time by prolonging the investigation and making more buys."

The solution to all of this madness in drug sentencing has nothing to do with reducing the sentences for crack cocaine possession, or increasing the sentences for powder cocaine possession, to eliminate disparity and racism. Nor does it have anything to do with reducing mandatory minimum sentences or eliminating stacking. And neither does it have anything to do with making or not making any sentencing guidelines retroactive.

The war on drugs is a monstrous evil that has undoubtedly ruined more lives than drugs themselves. Thousands of Americans (about 93 percent of them men) are locked in cages where they face rape, humiliation, financial ruin, the loss of the their families, and a criminal record that will haunt them the rest of their life for the "crime" of possessing or selling a substance the government doesn't approve of.

Does this mean that prisoners who have committed violence to person or property in conjunction with their drug "crime" should be released? Not at all. Persons who commit acts of violence—whether drugs are involved are not—should suffer the consequences of their actions. But anyone in prison merely for possessing or "dealing" drugs should be released immediately, as should everyone else imprisoned for victimless crimes.

15

Three Views on the Drug War
(Future of Freedom Foundation Commentaries, January 10, 2012)

One of the most important things the Republican congress-man and presidential candidate Ron Paul said as a guest on the *Tonight Show* with Jay Leno recently was what he said during his backstage interview after the show was over.

The first thing Representative Paul was asked was a question submitted by a Jay Leno Facebook fan: "Are you gonna legalize marijuana?" His answer was that he was "not going to enforce any federal laws against marijuana." He went on to say that there was "no authority in the Constitution to regulate anything a person puts in their body."

In a Ron Paul interview with Jon Stewart back in October, there was an omitted clip that appeared only online. In that segment, Dr. Paul said he fears the war on drugs more than he fears the drugs themselves. He not only said the war on drugs violates civil liberties, but also made the case for freedom of choice when it comes to drug use, including the freedom to use heroin.

That wasn't the first time that candidate Paul had talked about heroin use. During the Republican presidential debate in South Carolina back in May, Fox's Chris Wallace brought up the subject of Paul's belief that the federal government should stay out of people's personal habits. He then specifically mentioned the legalization of drugs and then bluntly asked Paul, "Are you suggesting that heroin and prostitution are an exercise of liberty?" Paul said "Yes," and then made the case that Americans don't need government prohibitions against heroin to keep them from using heroin.

Although Paul is correct in emphasizing that the Constitution nowhere authorizes the federal government to regulate the personal habits of Americans, whenever he talks about the drug war he ultimately focuses on how the decision to use or not use drugs is a matter of individual liberty and personal freedom.

He is simply expressing the libertarian view of the drug war. Although using hallucinogenic drugs may be immoral, sinful, unhealthy, destructive, a waste of money, a dumb thing to do, or all of the above, in a free society people must have the freedom to use or abuse drugs for freedom's sake.

The libertarian view is simple and consistent: Since it is not the business of government to prohibit, regulate, restrict, license, limit, or otherwise control what someone wants to smoke, snort, sniff, inject, or swallow, then there should be no laws whatever regarding the buying, selling, possessing, using, growing, processing, or manufacturing of any drug for any reason. Therefore, not only marijuana, but all drugs should be decrimialized—immediately; all drug laws should be repealed—immediately; and all those imprisoned solely for drug crimes should be released—immediately.

Although there is a place for practical or utilitarian arguments about how the war on drugs has unnecessarily made criminals out of too many otherwise law-abiding Americans, clogged the judicial system, and expanded the prison population, and how it has cost the taxpayers hundreds of billions of dollars with no substantial benefits to show for it, increased the size and scope of government, and violated the financial privacy and civil liberties of people who did not use or traffick in drugs, the libertarian view of the drug war is ultimately a moral or philosophical one.

The opposite view of the drug war is that of prohibition. Although there is still a Prohibition Party in the United States and a candidate for president from the party every four years who runs on a platform of bringing back alcohol prohibition, most Americans—even those who are strictly religious or who don't drink alcohol—recoil from the thought of turning back the clock to the Prohibition era. Yet, the same people see nothing inconsistent about the prohibition of drugs.

It doesn't matter what their political persuasion, liberals, conservatives, Democrats, and Republicans all generally support prohibition when it comes to drugs. Although some may argue that using drugs is immoral and others may argue that using drugs is destructive to one's health, their arguments are really the same: Instead of individuals deciding on whether to use drugs, it is the state—in collusion with legislators, regulators, nanny statists, drug warriors, paternalists, bureaucrats, and busybodies—that decides which drugs should be legal for use.

But a supposed moral and healthy society is not necessarily a free society. In a free society the individual makes his own decisions about his health and lifestyle; in an authoritarian society the state thinks it knows best how to make those decisions. In a free society the individual is free to make bad decisions; in an authoritarian society the state thinks it knows best what decisions people should make. In a free society the individual person is responsible for the consequences of his actions; in an authoritarian society the state thinks it knows best what actions people should take.

In between the libertarian view of the drug war (freedom) and the prohibitionist view of the drug war (tyranny) is a confusing mass of inconsistency, hypocrisy, and nonsense.

There is no disputing that the war on drugs has utterly failed. It has failed to prevent drug abuse and drug overdoses. It has failed to keep drugs out of the hands of addicts and teenagers. It has failed to reduce drug trafficking and violence. It has failed to reduce drug use and the demand for drugs. It has failed to respect natural rights and civil liberties. It has failed to be practical and cost effective.

But in spite of recognizing some of the drug war's shortcomings, advocates of a "third way" when it comes to the drug war still believe in some kind of a nanny state to monitor the behavior of its citizens. They are really just partial prohibitionists.

Some want the drug war to be better managed. Others want to focus on drug traffickers instead of drug users. Some want to legalize medical marijuana, but not all marijuana. Others want to decriminalize marijuana use, but not cocaine use. Some want to legalize certain drugs, but only so they can be taxed. Others want to legalize certain drugs, but only if they are regulated by the government.

Individual liberty and personal freedom are the farthest things from the minds of these partial prohibitionists.

Libertarians, as well as civil libertarians and strict constitutionalists who share the libertarian view on the drug war, must remain diligent and uncompromising in defense of absolute drug freedom. Constitutional, practical, utilitarian, emotional, medical, empirical, and common-sense arguments for drug freedom, although they have a time and a place, must always yield to the moral and philosophical ones. That is not to say that partial drug freedom is not preferable to outright prohibition or that steps toward drug freedom—such as decriminalizing small amounts of marijuana—are bad ideas. But it should never be forgotten that all people everywhere have the natural, moral, and civil right to buy, sell, grow, manufacture, or ingest whatever substance they choose for whatever reason they choose, including—are you listening Jon Stewart and Chris Wallace?—heroin.

16

Should Christians Support the War on Drugs?
(*LewRockwell.com*, March 13, 2012)

Televangelist and founder of the Christian Coalition Pat Robertson, with whom I have major theological, philosophical, and political differences, recently said something that even I must acknowledge was important, truthful, and courageous.

Speaking about the criminal justice system on his "700 Club" television program, Robertson remarked that it was a "shocking statistic" that the United States has "the highest rate of incarceration of any nation on the face of the Earth." Then he said something few "law and order" conservatives—and especially Christian conservatives—would dare to say: "More and more prisons, more and more crime. It's just shocking, especially this business about drug offenses. It's time we stop locking up people for possession of marijuana. We just can't do it anymore...You don't lock 'em up for booze unless they kill somebody on the highway."

This is not the first time that Robertson has come out for the legalization of marijuana. Back in 2010, he raised the same points:

> We're locking up people that have taken a couple puffs of marijuana and next thing you know they've got 10 years with mandatory sentences.
>
> I'm not exactly for the use of drugs, don't get me wrong, but I just believe that criminalizing marijuana, criminalizing the possession of a few ounces of pot, that kinda thing it's just, it's costing us a fortune and it's ruining young people. Young people go into prisons, they go in as youths and come out as hardened criminals. That's not a good thing.

Not everyone at the Christian Broadcasting Network, however, shared Robertson's views. A spokesman claimed that Robertson "did not call for the decriminalization of marijuana." He was merely "advocating that our government revisit the severity of the existing laws because mandatory drug sentences do harm to many young people who go to prison and come out as hardened criminals."

Pat Robertson is exactly correct on the subject of marijuana possession. This doesn't necessarily mean that he favors the legalization of other drugs or even the fully legalized cultivation, sale, and distribution of marijuana, but it does raise the important question of whether Christians should support the war on drugs.

Although I am a theological and cultural conservative, and neither advocate nor condone the use of mind-altering, behavior-altering, or mood-altering substances, I believe that Christians shouldn't support the government's war on drugs any more than they should support the government's wars on poverty, obesity, dietary fat, cholesterol, cancer, and tobacco.

Not only do I not use what are classified by the government as illegal drugs, wouldn't use them if they were legal, and would prefer that no one else do so whether they are legal or illegal, I would rather see people use drugs than the government wage war on them for doing so.

As a believer in moral absolutes, I consider the use of any drug for any reason other than because of a medical necessity to be dangerous, destructive, and immoral, but I also consider the government's war on drugs to be dangerous, destructive, and immoral.

As an adherent to the ethical principles of the New Testament, I regard drug abuse to be a vice, a sin, and an evil that Christians should avoid even as they avoid supporting the government's war on drugs.

As a Christian, I oppose root and branch every facet of the government's war on drugs just as much as I oppose the use of drugs themselves.

Yes, I know I am being redundant. But that's because some

Christians still just don't get it. So let me make myself perfectly clear: drugs are bad. Smoking crack is evil. Getting high on marijuana cigarettes or brownies is a vice. Snorting cocaine is destructive. Shooting up with heroin is sinful. Swallowing ecstasy is immoral. Injecting yourself with crystal meth is dangerous. But none of these things means that there should be a law against doing any of them. And it is a myth that those who favor marijuana legalization or drug decriminalization just want to get high without being hassled by the police. Pat Robertson certainly doesn't. And I certainly don't either.

There are many reasons why Christians should not support the war on drugs.

Constitutionally, the federal government has no authority whatsoever to regulate drugs, let alone criminalize their manufacture, sale, and use. Just like the government has no authority to control what Americans choose to eat, drink, smoke, inject, absorb, snort, sniff, inhale, swallow, or otherwise ingest into their bodies.

Philosophically, it is not the purpose of government to be a nanny state that monitors the behavior of its citizens. It is simply not the purpose of government to protect people from bad habits or harmful substances or punish people for risky behavior or vice. Drug prohibition is impossible to reconcile with a limited government.

Pragmatically, the war on drugs should be ended because it is a complete and total failure. As I have pointed out many times, the war on drugs has failed to prevent drug abuse, reduce drug trafficking, or reduce the demand for drugs. It has ruined more lives than drugs themselves.

Practically, the war on drugs should be ended because all it does is clog the judicial system, unnecessarily swell prison populations, foster violence, corrupt law enforcement, hinder legitimate pain treatment, and unreasonably inconvenience retail shopping.

Medically, the war on drugs is misguided. In a study by the Independent Scientific Committee on Drugs published in the prestigious medical journal *The Lancet*, it was alcohol that ranked as the "most harmful drug," beating out heroin, crack cocaine, and ecstasy. And then there is the fact that tens of thousands of people die every year from prescription drugs and reactions to over-the-counter drugs like aspirin.

Financially, the costs of drug prohibition far outweigh the benefits. According to a 2010 study by the Cato Institute, spending on the drug war tops $41 billion a year. What have we gotten for this except the militarization of the police, the erosion of civil liberties, and the destruction of financial privacy?

Theologically, and most importantly, there is no warrant in the New Testament for Christians to support a war on drugs by the government. And it is the theological reason that I wish to focus on.

Christian Inconsistency and Hypocrisy

It is unfortunate that many Christians—and probably most conservative Christians—are supporters of legislation to prohibit the doing of things like taking drugs that libertarians would consider to be victimless crimes and therefore not crimes at all. This support is inconsistent and hypocritical.

Getting stoned on crack or tripping out on LSD is, of course, not mentioned in the Bible. The closest thing would be getting drunk, which is definitely condemned:

> Let us walk honestly, as in the day; not in rioting and drunkenness, not in chambering and wantonness, not in strife and envying (Romans 13:13)

> And be not drunk with wine, wherein is excess; but be filled with the Spirit; (Ephesians 5:18)

Yet, every bad thing that could be said regarding drug abuse could also be said of alcohol abuse—and then some.

Alcohol abuse is a factor in many drownings, home, pedestrian, car, and boating accidents, suicides, fires, violent crimes, child abuse cases, sex crimes, divorces, and fetal abnormalities. The number one killer of young people under twenty-five is alcohol-related automobile accidents. Alcohol abuse is one of the leading causes of premature deaths in the United States. It can also be a contributing factor in cases of cancer, mental illness, and cirrhosis of the liver.

Although the manufacture and sale of alcohol is heavily regulated by the federal and state governments, anyone is free to drink as much as he wants in his own home without fear of reprisal. Except for a small number who want to return to the days of Prohibition, Christians are woefully inconsistent and hypocritical when they call for the government to wage war on drugs but not on alcohol.

Sin and Crime

We know that murder, robbery, and rape are both crimes and sins, but everything the state or the authorities brand a crime is not necessarily a sin. This has been true in all ages.

In the Old Testament, the Hebrew midwives were commanded by the state to kill any newborn sons (Exodus 1:16). But because "the midwives feared God," they "did not as the king of Egypt commanded them, but saved the men children alive" (Exodus 1:17).

In the book of Daniel, we read that King Nebuchadnezzar "made an image of gold" (Daniel 3:1) and decreed that when the music started, everyone was to "fall down and worship the golden image" (Daniel 3:5). The three Hebrew children— Shadrach, Meshach, and Abednego—defied the king and refused to worship the golden image, for which they were cast into a burning fiery furnace (Daniel 3:18-20).

In the New Testament, the apostles Peter and John were imprisoned by the authorities for preaching and then brought before them and commanded "not to speak at all nor teach in the name of Jesus" (Acts 4:18). But instead of being in subjection, they replied: "Whether it be right in the sight of God to hearken unto you more than unto God, judge ye. For we cannot but speak the things which we have seen and heard" (Acts 4:19-20).

After this incident, some apostles were again brought before the authorities and asked: "Did not we straitly command you that ye should not teach in this name? And, behold, ye have filled Jerusalem with your doctrine, and intend to bring this man's blood upon us" (Acts 5:28). It was then that the apostles uttered the immortal line: "We ought to obey God rather than men" (Acts 5:29).

No Christian could read these accounts and say with a straight face that everything the state labels a crime is a sin. The Bible is very clear about what sin is. Sin is "whatsoever is not of faith" (Romans 14:23). Sin is transgressing the divine law (1 John 3:14). Sin is knowing to do good and doing it not (James 4:17). Sin is "all unrighteousness" (1 John 5:17). But if not all crimes are sins, then why are some Christians often so quick to nod in agreement when it comes to the state's war on drugs? The only explanation is that some Christians think that disobeying the state is itself a crime. They have made the state into a god. They have violated the First Commandment.

But taking drugs to get high is a sin, says the Christian drug warrior. Agreed. But should it be a crime?

Victimless Crimes

There is another side of sin/crime coin: not all sins are crimes. If they were, then everyone would be in trouble, Christians included, for the Bible says that "there is not a just man upon earth, that doeth good, and sinneth not" (Ecclesiastes 7:20). Saying that not all sins are crimes is just a Christian way of rephrasing what was said by the nineteenth-century classical liberal political philosopher Lysander Spooner:

> Vices are those acts by which a man harms himself or his property.
>
> Crimes are those acts by which one man harms the person or property of another.
>
> Vices are simply the errors which a man makes in his search

after his own happiness. Unlike crimes, they imply no malice toward others, and no interference with their persons or property.

No Christian would be in favor of criminalizing all sins. Not when the Bible says that "the thought of foolishness is sin" (Proverbs 24:9). Why, then, are some Christians so quick to applaud making some sins criminal just because the state happens to select them and not others?

There are two types of victimless crimes: the immoral and the moral. This is because God's law never changes. What the state declares to be a crime one day can be declared not to be a crime the next day. Immoral victimless crimes are crimes that are sins in the eyes of God even if the state one day declares them not to be crimes; moral victimless crimes are crimes that have been labeled as such by the state that are not, in and of themselves, sins in the eyes of God. But either way, every crime needs a victim.

Christian Ignorance

The Christian's ultimate rule of faith is the New Testament, not canon law, church tradition, church councils, papal decrees, creeds and confessions, the musings of televangelists, the opinions of theologians, the sermons of some popular preacher, denominational pronouncements, church covenants, and not even the Old Testament, although "whatsoever things were written aforetime were written for our learning, that we through patience and comfort of the Scriptures might have hope" (Romans 15:4).

There is no support in the New Testament for the idea that Christians should seek legislation that would criminalize victimless acts like taking drugs. Specific sins are mentioned that are in fact crimes, like murder (Romans 1:29), stealing (Ephesians 4:28), rioting (Romans 13:13), and extortion (1 Corinthians 6:10). But what we mainly see in the New Testament are admonitions about how Christians should behave:

Recompense to no man evil for evil. Provide things honest in the sight of all men. (Romans 12:17)

As we have therefore opportunity, let us do good unto all men. (Galatians 6:10)

Let no corrupt communication proceed out of your mouth. (Ephesians 4:29)

Abstain from all appearance of evil. (1 Thessalonians 5:22)

Then there are the lists of vices for Christians to avoid: adultery, fornication, uncleanness, inordinate affection, covetousness, anger, malice, blasphemy, filthy communication, effeminacy, idolatry, hatred, strife, reveling, witchcraft, evil speaking, envy, lying, and bitterness. Should people be fined or jailed for these things if they don't result in harm to someone else's person or property? Then why should they be fined or jailed for taking drugs?

There are no indications anywhere in the New Testament that Christians should seek or support making these things crimes. Where did the Apostle Paul, in his travels throughout the Roman Empire, ever express support for any type of legislation? When did he ever tell people who were not Christians how they should live their lives? It is unfortunate that many Christians who support the drug war would support legislation against almost anything they considered to be bad behavior—as long as it stopped short of their particular vice.

Christian Failure

It is not the purpose of Christianity to change society as a whole outwardly; it is the purpose of Christianity to change men as individuals inwardly. The Christian is in the world, but not of the world. He is to "have no fellowship with the unfruitful works of darkness, but rather reprove them" (Ephesians 5:11), not legislate against them. The Christian is to "live peaceably with all men" (Romans 12:18). Christians are to pray for those in authority that they (Christians) "may lead a quiet and peaceable life" (1 Timothy 2:2). The attitude of the Christian should be to mind his "own business" (1 Thessalonians 4:11) and not be "a busybody in other men's matters" (1 Timothy 4:15).

I believe that Christians have for the most part failed to fulfill their calling. Instead of making converts and instructing them in the biblical precepts of Christian living, they turn to the state to criminalize what they consider to be immoral behavior. Instead of changing people's minds about what is and what is not acceptable in society, they seek to use the state to change people's behavior. Instead of being an example to the world, they want to use the state to make the world conform to their example. Instead of educating themselves and other Christians about what is appropriate behavior, they rely on the state to make that determination. Instead of being the salt of the earth and the light of the world, they want the state to assume those roles. Instead of minding their own business, they mind everyone else's business.

Christian Folly

Christians are making a grave mistake by looking to the state to legislate morality. The state is no real friend of religion, and especially not of Christianity. Why do so many Christians defend, support, and make excuses for the state, its politicians, its legislation, and its wars? Why would Christians even think of looking to the state to enforce their moral code?

It is not the purpose of Christianity to use force or the threat of force to keep people from sinning. Christians who are quick to criticize Islamic countries for prescribing and proscribing all manner of behavior are very inconsistent when they support the same thing here. A Christian theocracy is just as unscriptural as an Islamic theocracy.

But instead of greeting with a healthy dose of skepticism the state's latest pronouncement about what substance needs to be banned, regulated, or taxed, many Christians wholeheartedly embrace it. Instead of looking internally for funding, they look to the state to fund their faith-based initiatives.

Most Christians simply have too high a view of the state. They are too quick to rely on the state, trust the state, and believe the state. Sure, they may criticize the state because it permits abortion, but they generally fail to discern the state's true nature.

Economist William Anderson has summed it up nicely:

> Most conservative Christians abhor libertarianism because they see it as promoting a permissive lifestyle, from abortion to taking drugs. Yet, what they fail to understand is that the restrictive, prohibition-oriented state that they are trying to create (and also preserve) is much more likely to take away all liberties than a state that gives people permission to live as they wish.

Conclusion

Although drug abuse is a great evil, the war on drugs is an even greater evil. Christians should not compound these evils by supporting a war on behavior the government doesn't approve it. If getting high is against God's law. Then, as columnist Charley Reese once said: "Presumably God will enforce his own laws. You won't find in the Christian Bible any passage that says the responsibility for enforcing God's laws rests with the secular state." And furthermore:

> Christianity is a personal religion, not a tribal or state religion. If you wish to be a Christian, then you have a personal obligation to obey the commands of the Christian religion. Whether someone else does or does not is of no concern to you. You can be a devout, scrupulously pure Christian in the midst of the most outrageous sinners. Your obligation is to obey God's commandments, not to compel someone else to do it.

It is simply not biblical to promote legislation or crusades to punish sin that does not aggress against person or property. The proper approach to the problem of drug abuse was wisely spoken by the late economist Ludwig von Mises:

> He who wants to reform his countrymen must take resource to persuasion. This alone is the democratic way of bringing about changes. If a man fails in his endeavors to convince other people of the soundness of his ideas, he should blame his own disabilities. He should not ask for a law, that is, for compulsion and coercion by the police.

That is the spirit of New Testament Christianity. It's just unfortunate that it is a nonreligious Jew expressing such an opinion instead of the typical evangelical Christian.

17

The Drug War: Cui Bono?

(Future of Freedom Foundation Commentaries, May 17, 2012)

Cui bono, a maxim of Cassius quoted by Cicero meaning "who benefits?" or "to whose advantage?" is a useful principle when investigating political assassinations, conspiracy theories, mysterious deaths—and the war on drugs.

The war on drugs, which actually began in the United States before World War I with the passage of a series of federal anti-narcotics laws, was officially declared by Richard Nixon in 1971. It was expanded by Ronald Reagan and the "Just Say No" campaign of the 1980s, reached ridiculous heights under George W. Bush's Combat Methamphetamine Epidemic Act of 2005, and continues in 2012 under Barack Obama and his crackdown on medical marijuana dispensaries.

Although the war on drugs is a war on a victimless crime that is not sanctioned by the Constitution, has ruined countless lives, has cost untold billions, and is a failure in every respect, it continues unabated, full-steam ahead. It will not even be an issue in the 2012 presidential and congressional elections.

True, medical marijuana is now legal in sixteen states (Alaska, Arizona, California, Colorado, Delaware, Hawaii, Maine, Michigan, Montana, Nevada, New Jersey, New Mexico, Oregon, Rhode Island, Vermont, and Washington) and the District of Columbia, and there is legislation to that effect pending in a dozen more, but drug warriors have hardly noticed.

I see four reasons why.

First, marijuana remains a Schedule I controlled substance. The federal government still considers growing, distributing, or possessing marijuana in any capacity to be a violation of federal law regardless of any state laws to the contrary.

Second, states that have to some degree legalized marijuana

for medical use all have numerous restrictions, rules, and regulations regarding the prescribing, possession, growing, buying, and selling of marijuana. In addition, there are fees to pay, paperwork to fill out, fingerprints to be taken, cards to be issued, dispensaries to be inspected, and background checks to be done.

Third, the use of marijuana—for medical reasons or not—is still viewed very negatively. And of course, the use of drugs such as cocaine, LSD, and heroin is disparaged even more.

Fourth, there is almost universal support for the drug war among Democrats, Republicans, Catholics, Protestants, police, preachers, physicians, and housewives; that is, among the vast majority of Americans. The only two major groups who think the contrary are libertarians and college students. There is only one member of Congress that I know of who has absolutely and consistently opposed the drug war—Rep. Ron Paul (R-Tex.).

There is no logical or sane reason that a policy like the war on drugs that is so blatantly unconstitutional, that is such a miserable failure, that has so eroded civil liberties, that has so destroyed financial privacy, and that has fostered so much violence should be supported by so many people.

Some people support the drug war because they view getting high on drugs as immoral. Others favor prohibition because they consider narcotics to be addictive. Still others focus on the dangers of ingesting illegal drugs. They are all, of course, inconsistent, since they rarely call for outright bans on alcohol, tobacco, or bungee jumping.

But there are other groups of people who support the drug war for reasons totally unrelated to whether illegal drug use is immoral, addictive, or dangerous. Persons in these groups may even think that taking drugs is all of those things and more, and believe that most drugs should be banned, but that is not the main reason that they support the drug war.

Some people support the war on drugs because they have something to gain from it. They are advantaged in some way by it.

The first group who benefits from the war on drugs is drug

dealers. They may not use drugs themselves, but they know a good investment when they see it. The reason that the price of some drugs is so astronomical is that drugs are illegal. The penalties for drug smuggling are severe, the risks to life and limb are great, but the potential profits are incredible. Joaquin "El Chapo" Guzman Loera, the head of the Mexican Sinaloa drug cartel, recently said that he owed his fortune to the U.S. war on drugs:

> I couldn't have gotten so stinking rich without George Bush, George Bush Jr., Ronald Regan and even El Presidente Obama, none of them have the cojones to stand up to all of the big money that wants to keep this stuff illegal. From the bottom of my heart, I want to say "Gracias Amigos" I owe my whole empire to you.

The second group who benefits from the war on drugs is alcohol distributors. Illicit drugs are a threat to their sales of beer, wine, and spirits. Purveyors of alcohol are afraid that people might substitute smoking marijuana at home while watching the playoffs for drinking beer at the local sports bar. In 2010, a ballot initiative in California called Proposition 19, the Regulate, Control & Tax Cannabis Act, would have made it legal for individuals to possess a maximum of one ounce of marijuana and for authorized retailers to sell it to those 21 and older. Although the initiative was defeated, it is interesting that the California Beer & Beverage Distributors spent money in the state to oppose the initiative.

The third group who benefits from the war on drugs is the prison industry, including private prison corporations. One of the most evil things about the war on drugs is that it has unnecessarily swelled the prison population. More than half of the federal prison population and about 20 percent of the state prison population are imprisoned because of the drug war. In 2008, California prison guards spent more than a million dollars to defeat a proposition that would have sent some nonviolent drug offenders into treatment rather than to prison. The California Correctional Supervisors Organization gave $7,500 toward defeating Proposition 19.

The fourth group who benefits from the war on drugs is law enforcement. Another evil thing about the war on drugs is that it makes criminals out of too many otherwise law-abiding Americans. According to the FBI's latest report, "Crime in the United States," more than 1.6 million Americans were arrested on drug charges in 2010, with almost half of those arrests just for marijuana possession. How fewer and smaller law-enforcement agencies would be without the war on drugs. Oh, and the California Narcotics Officers' Association, the California Police Chiefs Association, the California Peace Officers Association, and the California District Attorney Association all contributed toward defeating Proposition 19. (A growing exception to law-enforcement support of the drug war is the organization Law Enforcement against Prohibition [LEAP], an international association of criminal-justice professionals who favor a repeal of drug-prohibition laws.)

The fifth group who benefits from the war on drugs is the federal Drug Enforcement Administration (DEA). The DEA made almost 31,000 arrests last year. It has 10,000 employees in 226 offices organized in 21 divisions throughout the United States and 83 foreign offices in 63 countries around the world. The DEA even employs 300 chemists and 124 pilots. These government parasites owe everything they do to the war on drugs. And don't forget the state DEA parasites.

And then there are physicians and the pharmaceutical industry, state and federal prosecutors, judges and lawyers, the CIA and the FBI, the drug-testing and addiction-recovery industries, and any group receiving federal funds for anti-drug campaigns.

Cui bono?

More individual persons and organizations than you might think.

18

Twelve Victims of the Drug War

(Future of Freedom Foundation Commentaries, June 19, 2012)

According to the Centers for Disease Control, 37,792 people died from drug overdoses in 2010. That exceeds the number of Americans killed in car accidents (35,080). It was the second year in a row that drug deaths outnumbered traffic fatalities.

The majority of those deaths were caused, not by heroin or cocaine, but by prescription opioid painkillers such as oxycodone (OxyContin) and hydrocodone (Vicodin).

There is no question that abusing drugs—legal or illegal—can be dangerous, destructive, and deadly. Taking certain drugs can be addictive, result in financial ruin, and lead to crime to support one's habit. I would even agree with those who consider drug abuse to be evil, immoral, and sinful.

But it's not just drugs that have their victims. The War on Drugs has many victims as well. Not in any particular order, here are twelve victims of the Drug War.

The first victim of the Drug War is the Constitution. There is absolutely no authority given to the federal government by the Constitution to wage a war against drugs, concern itself with any substance that Americans choose to ingest, or ban the manufacture, sale, or use of any substance. None whatsoever. If marijuana, cocaine, ecstasy, crystal meth, crack, heroin, speed, and LSD were the deadliest substances known to man, the federal government would still have no more authority to ban them than it would have to ban baseball, hot dogs, or apple pie. When the government decided to prohibit the "manufacture, sale, or transportation of intoxicating liquors" during the Prohibition era, the Eighteenth Amendment to the Constitution had to be adopted first. The same should be true of drug prohibition.

The **second victim** of the Drug War is the English language. Two of the most despised occupations are drug trafficker and drug dealer. Yet how ridiculous it would sound if Americans spoke of spinach traffickers and apple dealers. Drug traffickers and drug dealers are middlemen who bring together producers and consumers. We may not like the products, but we can choose not to purchase them. It is only because of drug prohibition that drug traffickers and dealers are usually such unsavory characters.

The **third victim** of the Drug War is the American taxpayer. According to a Cato Institute White Paper titled "The Budgetary Impact of Ending Drug Prohibition," the Drug War costs American taxpayers $41.3 billion per year. And what do they get for their money? The erosion of civil liberties, the destruction of financial privacy, and the erection of a police state. The financial and human costs of the Drug War far exceed any of its supposed benefits.

The **fourth victim** of the Drug War is common sense. Alcohol and tobacco kill more Americans than drugs, but any adult can purchase those substances and partake of them until he's dead and no one in the government will do anything to stop him. But possess sufficient quantities of a plant the government doesn't approve of and you will be locked in a cage. The federal government doesn't ban dangerous activities such as skydiving, bungee jumping, mountain climbing, mixed martial arts, jumping on trampolines, stock-car racing (Dale Earnhardt was killed in 2001), or drag racing (Scott Kalitta was killed in 2008). Yet the government bans certain drugs, and people support the Drug War, because drugs are dangerous. The number of babies born addicted to prescription painkillers has tripled in the last decade. Not crack and heroin babies, but Vicodin and OxyContin babies. Why hasn't the government banned those drugs? Oh, and the last time I checked, deaths from marijuana were still a big, fat zero.

The **fifth victim** of the Drug War is people who conduct business with cash. According to the IRS,

A business must file Form 8300 to report cash paid to it if

the cash payment is:

o Over $10,000,
o Received as:
    1. One lump sum of over $10,000,
    2. Two or more related payments that total in excess of $10,000, or
    3. Payments received as part of a single transaction (or two or more related transactions) that cause the total cash received within a 12-month period to total more than $10,000.
o Received in the course of trade or business,
o Received from the same payer (or agent), and
o Received in a single transaction or in two or more related transactions.

Try depositing more than $10,000 (or a daily aggregate in that amount) in cash in a bank and you are a suspected drug dealer. An insurance adjuster from New Jersey was transporting $20,000 in cash. It was confiscated by an overzealous cop during a traffic stop in Tennessee because, in the words of the cop, "On the street, a thousand-dollar bundle could approximately buy two ounces of cocaine." The motorist even explained and documented his active eBay bid on a car.

It doesn't even have to be an unusually large amount of cash. In 2009, Steve Bierfeldt, an employee of the political organization Campaign for Liberty, was detained in an airport after he sent a metal box with $4,700 in cash and checks through an X-Ray machine. He recorded the audio of his confrontation with the TSA, which included threats, insults, and repeated questions about where he obtained the money. He was told by the TSA that he would not be released if he refused to say why he was carrying so much cash. The TSA also threatened to notify the FBI and the DEA.

The sixth victim of the Drug War is people with allergies. The Combat Methamphetamine Epidemic Act, Title VII of the USA PATRIOT Improvement and Reauthorization Act of 2005, makes criminals of people who want Sudafed for their stuffy nose: Sudafed contains pseudoephedrine, which can be used to make crystal meth. In the House of Representatives, 207 out of 225 Republicans voted for the bill. Every Republican senator voted for the bill.

Diane Avera, a 45-year-old grandmother from Meridian, Mississippi, was stopped by the Demopolis, Alabama, police department for making an out-of-state Sudafed purchase in Alabama. She was arrested, abused, humiliated, and jailed for 40 days before being released on $51,000 bail. The police state is alive and well in America—thanks to the Drug War.

The seventh victim of the Drug War is crime. Every crime needs a victim. Not a potential victim or possible victim or a supposed victim, but an actual victim. Bad habits, poor judgment, dangerous activities, and vices are not crimes. The 19th-century classical-liberal political philosopher Lysander Spooner explained the difference: "Vices are those acts by which a man harms himself or his property. Crimes are those acts by which one man harms the person or property of another." Criminalizing drug use or drug possession distorts the nature of crime.

But drugs have other victims besides those who use them, do they not? John Stossel points out in his book *No, They Can't: Why Government Fails—But Individuals Succeed* that conservative talking head Bill O'Reilly has often cited a statistic that comes from the former HEW secretary Joseph Califano that 75 percent of child-abuse cases are caused by adults on drugs. But it turns out that the figure is based on an old survey in which the term "drugs" includes alcohol. It is actually legal alcohol that causes more harm than illegal drugs.

The eighth victim of the Drug War is law-abiding Americans whose lives or families are ruined because they were arrested for drugs and are in prison or will carry the stigma of a criminal record for the rest of their lives. In 2010, more than 1.6 million Americans were arrested on drug charges.

The ninth victim of the Drug War is law enforcement. The War on Drugs takes finite law-enforcement resources away from fighting real crime. It has militarized the local police. It has clogged the judicial system. It has swollen the prison population. It has corrupted law enforcement. It has resulted in ridiculous sting operations, as in Orange County, California, where the sheriff's department's crime lab manufactured crack cocaine for the police in Santa Ana to ensnare unsuspecting drug buyers. Thank God for the organization Law Enforcement Against Prohibition (LEAP).

The tenth victim of the Drug War is people who suffer with genuine pain, such as Miss Ann Lenhart of Dallas, Texas. She was arrested for trying to refill her Norco prescription after undergoing knee reconstruction surgery. When she arrived at her local CVS, a police officer escorted her outside and said, "We believe that you have forged your pain pill prescription and we are calling your doctor now. But I've worked with this pharmacist a number of times and he's never made a mistake." She was arrested, spent a night in jail, and was charged with the felony of obtaining a controlled substance by fraud. The charges were later dropped. Lenhart is suing CVS for false imprisonment and defamation.

The eleventh victim of the Drug War is doctors who prescribe pain medicine. Fewer doctors are going into pain management. And no wonder; it might eventually land them in court, as it did Dr. Cecil Knox. Dr. Knox was seeing patients in his clinic when more than a dozen helmeted, shielded, bullet-proof-vested federal agents burst through the doors with guns drawn. He was dragged out in handcuffs and leg irons. His assets were frozen and his bond was set at $200,000. He and several employees were handed a 313-count indictment, including charges of drug distribution resulting in death or serious bodily injury, prescription of drugs without a medical purpose, conspiracy, mail fraud, and health-care fraud. Jurors ultimately acquitted Knox of about 30 out of 69 charges, but they were deadlocked on the rest. Prosecutors then refiled the case with 95 charges, including racketeering, mail fraud, and multiple counts that his prescriptions of opioid medications were outside the scope of legitimate medical practice and led to death or serious bodily injury. He eventually surrendered his medical license and DEA registration number, pled guilty in a plea deal, and received five years' probation. So, as Maia Szalavitz wrote in a lengthy article about drug warriors who put the fear of prosecution into physicians who dare to treat pain,

> In their attempt to prevent prescription drug abuse, the DEA and the DOJ in effect have taken upon themselves the authority to regulate the practice of medicine, traditionally the province of the states. Worse, they have transformed disagreements about treatment decisions into criminal prosecutions, scaring physicians away from opioids and compounding the suffering of patients who have trouble getting the drugs they need to relieve their pain.

Did Dr. Knox help people in chronic pain? Certainly. Did he overprescribe pain killers? Perhaps. But did he drug anyone or did he force anyone to take drugs? (Ironically, the CIA and the military have done both.)

The twelfth victim of the Drug War is individual liberty. Ultimately, this is what it all comes down to. The War on Drugs is a war on individual liberty. It is a war on personal freedom. It is a war on private property. It is a war on the free market. It is a war on personal responsibility. It is a war on personal and financial privacy. It is a war on the Constitution. It is a war on federalism. It is a war on the free society.

The U.S. government's War on Drugs violates the natural, moral, civil, personal, and constitutional rights of all Americans to drug freedom. Whether drugs are used for medicinal, therapeutic, or recreational purposes—or just to get stoned out of your mind—doesn't matter. The right of an American to be left alone by his government as long as he does "anything that's peaceful" is the real victim in the Drug War.

19

Why the War on Drugs Should Be Ended
(Future of Freedom Foundation Commentaries, July 10, 2012)

The War on Drugs is a monstrous evil that has ruined more lives than drugs themselves. Taking drugs harms the person who partakes, but not those who abstain; the War on Drugs harms everyone, even those who abstain from taking drugs.

Yet the Drug War enjoys bipartisan support in Congress, is supported by the majority of Americans, is cheered by most religious people, is espoused by most parents with young children, is championed by liberals and conservatives alike, is encouraged by the majority of law-enforcement personnel, and is even defended by those who say they advocate "civil liberties" or "limited government."

But drugs are addictive. Yes, and so is caffeine.

But drugs are unhealthy. Yes, and so is high-fructose corn syrup.

But drugs are dangerous. Yes, and so is skateboarding.

But drugs are sinful. Yes, and so is adultery.

But drugs are a bad habit. Yes, and so is burping in public.

But drugs can be destructive. Yes, and so can tobacco smoking.

But drugs are a vice. Yes, and so is gluttony.

But drugs are immoral. Yes, and so is pornography.

But drugs harm children. Yes, and so does divorce.

But drugs may lead to premature death. Yes, and so may alcohol.

But drugs have societal costs. Yes, and so does obesity.

But drugs can lead to financial ruin. Yes, and so can using credit cards.

But drugs can kill. Yes, and so can prescription drugs.

But drugs can have unintended consequences. Yes, and so can sexual relations.

But drugs can lead to crime to support one's habit. Yes, and so can gambling.

But drugs have no redeeming value. Yes, and neither do Twinkies.

Why, then, do so many people support the War on Drugs? The main problem, I believe, is too little commitment to freedom and, concomitantly, too much faith in government. Americans who are not firmly committed to the freedom philosophy intuitively believe that when there is a problem, government action is the best or the only way to solve it.

In spite of all the evidence of the failures and destructiveness of the Drug War, drug warriors are intransigent when it comes to ending the Drug War.

Why should the Drug War be ended?

The War on Drugs should be ended not simply because it has failed to prevent drug abuse.

The War on Drugs should be ended not simply because marijuana has been found to have medical benefits.

The War on Drugs should be ended not simply because more people are killed by tobacco every year than are killed by all illegal drugs in the 20th century.

The War on Drugs should be ended not simply because smoking marijuana is less dangerous than drinking alcohol.

The War on Drugs should be ended not simply because it violates the Constitution.

The War on Drugs should be ended not simply because the D.A.R.E program has had, according to the GAO, "no statistically long-term effect on preventing youth illicit drug use."

The War on Drugs should be ended not simply because more people die from drugs prescribed and administered by physicians than from illegal drugs.

The War on Drugs should be ended not simply because it clogs the judicial system with noncrimes.

The War on Drugs should be ended not simply because it swells the prison population with nonviolent offenders.

The War on Drugs should be ended not simply because it

has failed to keep drugs away from teenagers.

The War on Drugs should not be ended not simply because it has lasted for more than 40 years with nothing lasting to show for it.

The War on Drugs should be ended not simply because other countries have legalized drugs with no increase in drug overdoses.

The War on Drugs should be ended not simply because it hinders legitimate pain management and turns doctors into criminals.

The War on Drugs should be ended not simply because it has failed to keep drugs out of the hands of addicts or to get them treatment.

The War on Drugs should be ended not simply because of its gross sentencing disparities.

The War on Drugs should be ended not simply because for the first half of our nation's history there were no prohibitions against any drug.

The War on Drugs should be ended not simply because it has made criminals out of hundreds of thousands of otherwise law-abiding Americans.

The War on Drugs should be ended not simply because it has devastated the black community.

The War on Drugs should be ended not simply because, according to a study published in the prestigious medical journal *The Lancet*, alcohol ranks as the "most harmful drug," beating out heroin, crack cocaine, and ecstasy.

The War on Drugs should be ended not simply because it has failed to stop the violence associated with drug trafficking.

The War on Drugs should be ended not simply because it has cost U.S. taxpayers billions of dollars.

The War on Drugs should be ended simply because there are many more activities that are much more dangerous than using drugs.

The War on Drugs should be ended not simply because it corrupts law enforcement.

The War on Drugs should be ended not simply because it is a war on a victimless crime.

The War on Drugs should be ended not simply because it has failed to reduce the demand for illicit drugs.

The War on Drugs should be ended not simply because its costs far exceed its benefits.

The War on Drugs should be ended because it is a war on the Constitution, federalism, and limited government. It is a war on personal responsibility and accountability. It is a war on individual liberty and private property. It is a war on personal and financial privacy. It is a war on peaceful activity and the right to be left alone if one is not aggressing against the person or property of another.

The War on Drugs should be ended, not gradually or partially, but immediately and completely. All drugs laws should be repealed. All prisoners incarcerated for drug possession should be released. All government agencies fighting the Drug War should be abolished.

If doesn't matter if all the bad things said about drugs are true. It doesn't matter if drugs are sinful and immoral. It doesn't matter if drugs are unhealthy and dangerous. It doesn't matter if drugs are inherently addictive. It doesn't matter if drug use leads to crime to support one's habit. It doesn't matter if drugs destroy homes and lives.

It doesn't matter if marijuana is a gateway drug. It doesn't matter if marijuana isn't beneficial for pain management.

It doesn't matter if someone you know died from a drug overdose. It doesn't matter if your kids are on drugs. It doesn't matter if you know someone who had a crack baby.

It doesn't matter if all the supposed negative effects of ending the Drug War actually do come to pass. It doesn't matter if millions more people would try drugs if they were legal. It doesn't matter if drug overdoses would increase. It doesn't matter if more people would become addicted to drugs. It doesn't matter if drugs would become cheaper and more readily available.

It doesn't matter if the Drug War can be "won." It doesn't matter if drug warriors have good intentions. It doesn't matter if some good might come from the Drug War. It doesn't matter if kids just say no to drugs. It doesn't matter if drug addicts get treatment. It doesn't matter if drug use among teens declines. It doesn't matter if demand for drugs shrinks.

It doesn't matter if the Drug War enjoys widespread bipartisan support. It doesn't matter if the majority of Americans back the Drug War. It doesn't matter if other countries believe in fighting the Drug War. It doesn't matter if physicians, psychiatrists, police, and social workers defend the Drug War.

It doesn't matter if advocates for medical marijuana just want to smoke pot for recreational purposes. It doesn't matter if proponents of drug decriminalization just want to get high. It doesn't matter if those who favor the legalization of drugs just want to get stoned out of their mind.

The War on Drugs should be ended because it is not really about drugs at all. It is about expanding the power and scope of the state. It is about politicians, bureaucrats, regulators, statists, nannies, and busybodies who tell Americans what they may and may not put into their mouths, noses, lungs, and veins.

The War on Drugs should be ended because it is a war on the free market, a free society, and freedom itself.